PERFECT PHRASES™

for

MANAGERS
AND
SUPERVISORS

second edition

**Hundreds of Ready-to-Use Phrases
for Overcoming Any Management Situation**

Meryl Runion

New York Chicago San Francisco Lisbon London Madrid Mexico City
Milan New Delhi San Juan Seoul Singapore Sydney Toronto

The McGraw·Hill Companies

Copyright © 2010 by The McGraw-Hill Companies, Inc. All rights reserved. Printed in the United States of America. Except as permitted under the United States Copyright Act of 1976, no part of this publication may be reproduced or distributed in any form or by any means, or stored in a database or retrieval system, without the prior written permission of the publisher.

3 4 5 6 7 8 9 10 11 12 13 14 15   QFR/QFR   1 9 8 7 6 5 4 3 2

ISBN   978-0-07-174231-3
MHID   0-07-174231-X

Library of Congress Cataloging-in-Publication Data

Runion, Meryl.
     Perfect phrases for managers and supervisors / Meryl Runion.—2nd ed.
         p.   cm.
     ISBN-13: 978-0-07-174231-3 (alk. paper)
     ISBN-10: 0-07-174231-X
     1. Management.   2. Management—Terminology.   3. Business communication.   I. Title.

     HD31.R83   2011
     658.4'5—dc22   2010010407

Trademarks: McGraw-Hill, the McGraw-Hill Publishing logo, Perfect Phrases, and related trade dress are trademarks or registered trademarks of The McGraw-Hill Companies and/or its affiliates in the United States and other countries and may not be used without written permission. All other trademarks are the property of their respective owners. The McGraw-Hill Companies is not associated with any product or vendor mentioned in this book.

McGraw-Hill books are available at special quantity discounts to use as premiums and sales promotions or for use in corporate training programs. To contact a representative, please e-mail us at bulksales@mcgraw-hill.com.

This book is printed on acid-free paper.

Contents

Contents

Contents

Chapter 6 Perfect Phrases to Ace the Interview You Conduct   49

Contents

Contents

Contents

Contents

Acknowledgments

I was thrilled to have the opportunity to rework this book and update the style of communication and the phrases to reflect current trends and demographic influence. So for that, I thank McGraw-Hill and my editor, Brian Foster.

Additional thanks to Evan Hodkins, who is a wordsmith after my own heart, and to Sharon Campbell, who contributed important content. And my husband, Bob, who contributes levity with an incredible sense of playfulness.

Introduction

There are so many management books on the market today that one might wonder why the world needs one more. The answer is that this book offers something the others don't. It's short and easy to navigate, and it addresses the specific challenges managers have shared with me during my years of management training.

The Challenges of an Accidental Manager

"Raise your hand if you manage or supervise one or more people," I asked my seminar attendees. A roomful of hands went up.

"Now keep your hand up if you've had management training." Not a single hand stayed up.

In a room of fifty managers, I'm lucky to have one who has received training in his or her vocation. Most make their jobs up as they go along. A Harris poll reported that up to 85 percent of managers are untrained. The informal surveys I conduct at my management seminars suggest this is a conservative figure.

Many people became managers the way I did. My first job was to assist on a major research project. Three months into the project, my manager quit. His manager called me in and said, "Meryl, I'm putting you in charge." I was too foolish and too flattered to decline. I almost drowned in my own incompetence.

Like me, most managers are left on their own to figure out how to manage without training or guidance. They learn through trial and error, with no understanding of procedure and proven techniques.

Trained managers face other challenges. Many find their management training focused on theory, systems, and processes more than practical interpersonal dynamics. Plus, the workplace is changing—and changing fast. Women, Generation Y, social media, and globalization are transforming the way we relate, influence, and succeed. There is a new dynamic of communication. That's why I'm revising this book only five years after its original publication. The phrases I recommended five years ago are not the phrases I recommend today.

Why Pick Perfect Phrases? The Importance of Planning Your Words

When managers don't have the words they need to say in a situation, they usually say nothing. I receive frequent letters from managers who tolerate inappropriate behavior from their employees. They ask me for the words to speak in situations they should have addressed years ago. When they find the words, they become willing to take action.

Other managers use aggressive words that create resistance, shut down communication, and backfire. Employees may respond to aggression in the short term, but forcefulness stifles productivity and can cause passive-aggressive blowback.

Even managers who have found a balance between passiveness and aggressiveness may not know how to use their words to develop the leadership potential of talented employees and to encourage them to take charge without taking over.

The Value of Scripting

Unless you are a management-communication natural, planning your words in advance will add to your success. Challenging situations result in tension, which creates fight-or-flight responses and passive and aggressive thinking. It's tough enough to recall phrases you planned in advance when you are triggered. It's almost impossible to think of options when you haven't planned.

Many people resist using scripted phrases because they're afraid they'll sound phony. If the new dynamics of communication are not instinctive to you, your preplanned phrases could sound unnatural at first. Hang in there. "Phony" clarity is more effective than "genuine" passiveness or aggressiveness.

Also, because the phrases are so appropriate, they often will seem natural even if they are rehearsed. These are the phrases you would have chosen yourself if only you had thought of them. Eventually you will wonder why you ever spoke any other way.

Perfect Phrases work.

How to Use This Book

One purpose of this book is for you to outgrow it. There are two approaches that will help you do that. One is to use this book as a quick reference for situations you face.

1. Review relevant sections before you speak.
2. Adapt the phrases to your need and personal style.
3. Practice your phrases before you use them.
4. After the conversation, review what you said and determine how you could have spoken more effectively.

A second approach is to use this as a practical crash course in management. Read *Perfect Phrases for Managers and Supervisors* from cover to cover. Perfect Phrases don't only teach you powerful wording; they also guide your action. This book gives you an overview of your management responsibilities and the words to use when you do your job.

If your specific issue is not covered in this book, please e-mail me at merylrunion@speakstrong.com. Let's make the dialogue reciprocal. If you have a favorite phrase that you find useful, please forward it for me to share with my newsletter subscribers ("The New Dynamics of PowerPhrases," speakstrong .com).

Thanks for reading my book. Let me know how I can be of service to you.

Chapter 1

The New Workforce Demographics Require New Dynamics of Communication

This is not "your father's Perfect Phrases book." That's because we don't work in our father's work environment. Many factors are changing the way we relate, influence, and succeed. These factors change the nature of power. What got us to the top in the past will hold us back in the future. The old model of management communication—top-down, controlled messages, paying lip service to employees while imposing force—doesn't work in this new world. We need new models and new phrasing for our new workplace demographics.

A Woman's Nation

Since 2008, women have officially outnumbered men in supervisory positions, and since October of 2009, they have taken predominance in the workplace as a whole.[1] The Shriver Report

---

[1]U.S. Department of Labor, Bureau of Labor Statistics, "Labor Force Statistics from the Current Population Survey. Women in the Labor Force: A Databook (2009 Edition)," bls.gov/cps/wlf-intro-2009.htm; and David Knowles, "Women Are Overtaking Men in the US," aolnews.com/article/women-are-overtaking-men-in-the-us/19260692.

declared the United States to be a woman's nation, with the postscript that "a woman's nation changes everything." While the report notes that not everyone experiences a feminized workplace culture, clearly the trend is toward acceptance and valuation of traditional women's characteristics. These are the qualities of collaboration, cooperation, and personalization of business interactions. Of course, men can and often do also embody these values. And many women don't. Some women struggle with a collaborative style, either because it is not natural to them or because they have spent decades adapting to a predominantly male communication workplace culture. Still, women are seen as the drivers of these trends. According to author Judy B. Rosener, women have shown themselves to be "far more likely than men to describe themselves as transforming subordinates' self-interest into concern for the whole organization and as using personal traits like charisma, work record, and interpersonal skills to motivate others."[2] This collaborative trend is expected to persist as women continue to grow in workforce predominance.

Generation Y

The youngest generation of workers is also pushing management toward a new communication dynamic. Generation Y is naturally conversational, informal, egalitarian, and personal. To inspire and motivate younger employees, managers are learning to develop their personal working relationships and deliver individual benefits to meet individual needs. The workers who

---

[2] Judy B. Rosener, "Ways Women Lead," *Harvard Business Review* 68, no. 6 (1990): 119–25.

make up this new generation expect their input, opinions, and desires to be acknowledged and for communication to be reciprocal. Most workers under age forty have never known a workplace without women managers and colleagues, and they are increasingly comfortable with a diversified workplace. Of course, this generation is also known for growing up with pervasive technology.

Globalization

Globalization is another transformative factor. We're talking to and working with people from all over the world whose cultures are unlike ours. No matter how much we homogenize, our diversity still has a way of showing up in expectations, reactions, and miscommunications. This requires collaborative dialogue.

Social Media

Social media is also having a dramatic effect on the workplace culture. Twitter, Facebook, and other forms of social media aren't just elements of the business climate to consider; they are drivers and reflectors of a new type of communication. We've gone from mass communication to masses of communicators. That alone is eroding the authoritarian communication model. Sound bites and messages in 140 characters or less are vogue. That feeds the desire for succinctness. Plus many employees are constantly logged on and linked in to their social networks. Meetings and events are peppered with audiences who text or tweet play-by-play analyses while the facilitator tries to keep their attention. And that's if the leader is engaging. If he or she is not engaging, the texts are unrelated to the event.

Social media also creates a whole new set of conversations that managers need to initiate. Our fathers' managers had to concern themselves with workers who played cards on company time. Today's managers monitor computer games and texting.

Stretch or Be Stretched

It's a stretch-or-be-stretched world out there. A manager who doesn't adapt to the dynamic new work climate will not be effective. Management theories are helpful, but managers also need concrete, tested communication action steps and phrases.

This book gives the accidental (and deliberate) manager immediate benefits by providing words to use in hundreds of contemporary management situations. They are quick, easy, and effective.

You'll find ready-to-use (and ready-to-adapt) phrases for every management situation. But first, we'll dive into the new dynamics of communication that provide a foundation for all the phrases included in these pages.

Chapter 2

The New Dynamics of Communication

The new way of talking can be summarized as five new dynamics, each with several components. Review them and apply them to the phrases in the subsequent chapters.

New Communication Dynamic #1: Be Gracefully Assertive

Say what you mean, and mean what you say without being mean when you say it.

As managers, it's our job to coordinate, not just let things haphazardly unfold. That includes giving clear directions, holding employees accountable, and addressing inevitable issues. Judging from the numerous questions I get from managers about situations they should have addressed literally years ago, many managers don't manage. I also get countless questions from employees whose managers are heavy-handed. Their managers aren't managing either—they're commanding. There's a fine balance between passive and aggressive communication that I used to refer to as being assertive. Now I add the adjective *gracefully* to that phrase to encourage a style of influence that doesn't overpower.

Here are some tips for being gracefully assertive.

1. Say what you mean. The new dynamics require us to be authentic. Although some people try to fake authenticity, the trend is toward genuine interaction between individuals. That means dropping roles. We can't put our manager hats on and become different people when we manage. It doesn't work to act like our image of what a manager should be. This new dynamic calls for us to retire role-playing and talk like real people communicating with other real people.

2. Mean what you say. We protect the power of our words when we do what we say we will. Our words are as powerful as our commitment to them. If we don't do what we say we will, after a while no one will believe anything we say. If we schedule meetings and consistently show up late, if we overbook ourselves and fall short on commitments, or if we talk about valuing diversity and inclusion yet act like we don't, it signals employees that our words are empty. They will assume our words are also empty when we speak about larger considerations such as opportunities, promotions, and loyalty.

3. Don't be mean when you say it. The word *assert* means "to state or express positively." I like that definition. But unfortunately *assert* also means "to act boldly or forcefully, especially in defending one's rights or stating an opinion." Too many managers berate employees and justify it with the assertiveness label. The concept of being gracefully assertive bypasses the aggressive connotation of self-expression.

Graceful assertiveness is part of a larger trend toward magnetic influence instead of coercive dominance. Stereotypical used-car salespeople can still make a living these days, but the most successful salespeople, marketers, and managers use the influence of attraction over the power of push.

New Communication Dynamic #2: Personalize

The saying "It's business; it's not personal" ignores the fact that because we are people, there is a personal aspect to all business transactions and communication. In fact, business communication is becoming increasingly personalized. The new dynamics of communication are person to person, engaged, and conversational. Networking and relationship-building skills are increasingly essential to success. Here are some personalization tips.

1. Acknowledge emotion. Change experts observe that when managers allow employees to express their emotions around change, they reach acceptance much more quickly.[1] While we don't want emotion to dominate our business interactions, a little acknowledgment goes a long way.

2. Be conversational. Communication is more than relaying information. It's an interchange of ideas between people. Communicate as a unique individual talking to anther unique individual rather than as an institution talking to another institution.

3. Illustrate ideas with living examples. Stories engage and examples illuminate ideas. For example, instead of passing around a dry list of social media policies, bring those policies to life with concrete examples that personalize the policies.

4. Monitor impersonal and utilitarian language. It may be accurate to refer to employees as human resources or human capital, but avoid speaking in ways that imply you see the people you manage in terms of their function instead of their

---

[1]Wendy Mack, *Leading After Layoffs*. Woodland Park, CO: Peak Publishing, 2009.

humanity. Terms like *associates* and *team member* are becoming popular to personalize the workplace culture.

5. Individualize. While every job has its standards and most policies apply universally, the current workplace culture demands that jobs and decisions allow room for individual adaptation. We need to balance standardization with individualization.

New Communication Dynamic #3: State Concisely

Whether you love or hate the microblogging phenomenon Twitter, don't ignore it. It has changed the world we manage. Twitter and similar sites both shape and reflect the nature of today's workforce—even beyond those who use it. Countless managers pontificate in the unabridged, encyclopedic, and uninspired narrative, and most employees these days want the pithy, concise version.

Obviously one way to develop the art of brevity is to learn your way around microblogging sites. It has taught me a lot about superfluous words. Twitter teaches users to say something meaningful in 140 characters or less. With that limitation imposed on them, Twitter users are forced to develop pithiness. Many of our employees practice the art of concise speaking through microblogging daily. Not every message can be condensed to 140 characters, nor should it be. But pithy words get heard. Anything we communicate that doesn't add to a message detracts from it. So choose your words wisely and speak concisely.

New Communication Dynamic #4: Synergize

The workplace isn't a democracy where the majority rules. It is a synergistic setting where the majorities and minorities and all else involved contribute to the structure. Well, the good ones are. Some workplaces still are rankist dictatorships, others are meritocracies, some are anarchies, and most are a mix of styles. However, the trend is decidedly in the direction of synergy—of operating by dynamically discovering, engaging, and incorporating input from all elements of a group or unit.

Rankism is the antithesis of synergy. Rankism describes the abuse of the power in rank. This can be blatant, but it also can show up in subtle ways like bloviating because you think those below you in the hierarchy are too captive to object or too stupid to be able to think for themselves. Rankism often is invisible to those with higher rank and glaringly obvious to everyone beneath them on the organizational chart. Synergistic managers honor expertise and insight where they find it, even if it comes from the janitor, mail clerk, or someone young enough to be their grandchild . . . or old enough to be their grandparent. Here are some synergistic principles.

1. Partner with the people you manage. The old rules viewed management as a series of impersonal transactions with obedient subordinates. In the new dynamics, we engage, include, and respond. We are a part of the team.

2. Pay individual attention to employees and adapt management styles, expectations, and job descriptions to their unique needs, talents, and styles. I have staff doing jobs I never imagined at the interview because I later discovered new talents.

3. Invite active employee participation in shaping policy through techniques like crowdsourcing and spaghetti management.

According to Wikipedia, crowdsourcing is "the act of outsourcing tasks to a group of people or community through an 'open call' asking for contributions." Think of architects who build without sidewalks until they see where people naturally walk. People vote with their feet for where those walks should be. Think of IBM, who developed its social media policy through a wiki that allowed for employee input. These decisions were made synergistically.

Spaghetti management engages employees in the formation and development of policy. While MBO (management by objective) creates focus, and MBWA (management by walking around) allows for casual interaction, MBTS (management by throwing spaghetti against the wall) empowers employees by inviting them to get involved in shaping vision and policy. When we managers throw out possibilities to see what sticks, it signals that we don't think employees are just order takers. It can take a while for staff to recognize what we're doing and to discover that not only do they really have useful input but we actually want to consider that input. Then, look out! The floodgates open.

4. Harmonize individual functions within each team. Open communication cultures will uncover ideas that conflict, need refining, and sometimes don't work. When people, ideas, and objectives collide, it isn't a simple matter of one being right and another being wrong. It can be a minor interface issue or a problem of elements being out of sync with one another. What is inappropriate in one context could be most appropriate in another. Harmonizing individual functions moves judgment to discernment, negation to discovery, and dismissal to distinction. It keeps us from shutting down something (or someone) that could be useful once it aligns with the whole and the whole aligns with it.

This process moves us from "no, but," to "yes, and." We find the gem inside the grumble, the insight inside the insult, and the creative outlet for the complaint. We acknowledge negativity and move to creative resolution and shared goals. We consider whether opposition indicates underlying issues. If it does, we uncover the issues and seek not an alternative perspective but an *expanded* one.

New Communication Dynamic #5: Dynamize

In computer speak, *dynamize* means transforming a static data structure into a dynamic one. In medical speak it means releasing the potency of a medicine. In management speak it means using language and communication strategies that impel (not compel) forward thinking, speaking, and action. The social dynamics of our culture demand momentum. Our younger employees grew up with lively television shows, technology, and lifestyles. Social media is all about momentum. Users have to respond quickly to catch a "wave." Here are some ways we can dynamize our communication.

1. Speak to what is happening in the present and then look ahead. My assistant, Ashley, once had a manager who said the same thing every day to motivate employees. It didn't. That's static. We maintain momentum when we respond to events right in front of us. We speak in a fresh, new way each moment.

2. Bridge the current moment to a visionary future filled with possibility. Too much emphasis on past mistakes kills momentum. Quickly shifting the focus toward possibilities creates a forward momentum. Talking about what we want more than what we don't want dynamizes conversation.

3. Adapt salutations and closings to message content and the recipients. Perfunctory salutations and closings in correspondence kill momentum. Ask yourself—did you choose the salutations and closings, or were they habitual and unconscious?

4. Welcome audibles. An audible is a football term for allowing the quarterback to change a play if the formation on the field indicates the need. Audibles allow for spontaneity, which creates momentum. Audibles give the feeling of being on a moving train. They also are necessary for productivity. Audibles empower our employees to adapt to a changing playing field.

While we're at it, we need to call our own audibles. An agenda is a great thing to have at a meeting, but we need to let our agendas serve us instead of us serving our agendas. If circumstances suggest we adapt the agenda, we allow for that.

5. Mentor. Empower employees to be their best selves and to develop and apply new skills. We want our employees to be better people after they communicate with us. We want our words to impel them to action and bring out the best in them.

The world of social media is filled with an abundance of "atta boys," "way-to-gos," and "you-go-girls." I'm not talking about cheap flattery or superficial positivity. I'm talking about words that elevate and help employees lead with their best selves. Of course, when we apply this communication dynamic, we're leading with *our* best, most resourceful selves.

We keep ourselves in so many boxes without realizing it. Imagine the momentum our dynamized communication will unleash. This style of communication opens up new ways of relating, influencing, and succeeding. It would be scary if it wasn't so exciting.

And that excitement moves us into our Perfect Phrases.

Chapter 3

Put Your Best Foot Forward: Perfect Phrases to Establish Your New Role

When I was in school, the new kids were usually either instantly popular or instantly unpopular. The tone they set the very first day stayed with them. The same is often true for new managers. That's why it's important to start by consciously creating the right momentum.

Whether we find ourselves supervising former peers, managing employees who wanted our position, or supervising a team that is used to slacking, we can expect to be tested. Some employees try to take advantage of our status as a new manager, and others may wait for us to fail. As a new manager, use Perfect Phrases to proactively address issues *before* they manifest. See which phrases help you start out on the right foot.

Perfect Phrases to Address Former Peers Who Are Now Employees

- If you were in my position now, what would you say to me?

- I need your help, understanding, and support in my new role as your manager because I can't do this without you.

- If our changing roles create bumps in the road, let's not pretend things are fine when they aren't. Let's talk openly so we can shape our new relationship deliberately and consciously.

- We used to complain about the manager before that was me. While I won't consider you disloyal if you find yourself talking among yourselves about me, I hope you will come to me directly with the issues.

- I know employees can turn management bashing into an art form. If you come to me instead, we can resolve issues before they become problems.

- I'm not comfortable criticizing upper management with you anymore. However, if you have an issue you need help with, I'm here for you. Instead of complaining about problems, we can address them.

- How do you feel about my being your manager?

- Do you have concerns about the change in our positions?

Perfect Phrases to Address Friends Who Are Now Employees

- If you were managing me instead of me managing you, what would you say to me now?

- My being your manager could be awkward because we are so close. What ideas do you have about how we can handle our new working relationship in light of our friendship?

- I value your friendship and that won't change. During business hours I am a manager first. Please work with me instead of taking it personally if my loyalty to my position seems to conflict with my loyalty to you as my friend.

- I am concerned that I might be suspected of favoritism toward you since we're friends. I will be careful to avoid that because it could divide the team. Please don't take it personally but also tell me if you think I take impartiality too far. I want to be fair to you and the others I manage.

- Outside of the office I am responsible to you as a friend. Inside the office I am responsible to you as your manager and to the team and the company. Please support me in balancing those responsibilities.

Perfect Phrases to Address Team Members Who Wanted the Promotion You Got

- I know you applied for this position. This is a tough situation for us both. Can I count on you to support me the way you would have wanted me to support you?

- If you had gotten the promotion instead of me and you were sitting across the table from me as my new manager, what would you say to me now?

- Do you want to talk about how you feel about my getting this promotion?

- If I hadn't gotten this promotion, I might feel some resentment toward the person who did. Is it possible that you feel that way?

- I understand your frustration and even anger. I think that's normal. How can we move past this and focus on our goals?

- Our new formal work relationship could be awkward for both of us. How do you see us working together as a team?

Perfect Phrases to Address the Acting Supervisor You Are Replacing

- If you were me stepping into this position, what would you ask the person leaving?

- What do you know that I need to know?

- Tell me three things you do managing this team that work really well, and three things to avoid.

- I need your help with the transition, because you know so much. Can I count on that?

- You're the expert on how to manage this team. Please tell me anything you think I need to know and give me a heads-up when I do things you wouldn't recommend.

- If people go to you instead of me, will you let me know? They're used to going to you, and I need to know what's going on.

- In the beginning you'll know more than I do, so it will make sense for people to go to you instead of me. Will you refer them to me anyway so we can transition quickly and smoothly? Thanks!

Perfect Phrases to Set the Initial Tone with Employees

These are phrases for you to use in a kickoff meeting with staff.

- If you were the new manager, how would you start?

- What have new managers done in the past that you liked?

- We'll continue doing business as usual. Before I make changes, I'll learn how things are done and why they are done the way they are.

- I have my own style and ways of working. Before I introduce changes, though, I'll study the existing culture so changes will be smooth.

- I'll observe you in your job at times to learn what you do. I may have a few questions or suggestions for you. Give me honest feedback to my suggestions so I can refine my understanding of what you do every day.

- We are a team, and as manager I am also a member of that team.

- I'll tell you about anything that affects you. Please be open with me too.

- I will meet with each of you privately to see how we can support each other.

Perfect Phrases for Your Initial Individual Meeting

Meetings with new employees help us get to know them and address issues before they become problems. Employees can prepare by reviewing their jobs and job descriptions.

- Before we meet, please prepare by reviewing your job description and your daily tasks, then evaluate how they match.

- What do you need from me as your manager?

- Are there obstacles to doing your job that I might be able to help you with?

- What motivates you?

- What have managers done in the past that worked well for you? Why did it work?

- What have managers done in the past that didn't work well for you? Why didn't it work?

- What advice do you have for me as your new manager?

- What aspects of your job do you think should be dropped?

- What would you like to see changed around here? Why?

- What is the best praise you ever received?

- Tell me about your dreams and career goals.

- Is there anything else you want to talk about that might help us work together better?

- Here's how I like to be updated. Does that work for you, or do you prefer another approach?

- I plan to copy you on e-mails that have info you need for background information. Unless I ask for specific input, you can assume you don't need to do anything about them. Even so, if something stands out that you want to comment on, I invite it.

- I have an open-door policy for emergencies. For routine questions that can wait, I appreciate your saving up several to minimize interruptions.

Perfect Phrases to Handle Questions You Can't Answer

No one expects the manager to have all the answers right out of the gate, except maybe ourselves. It doesn't impress anyone when we pretend to know things we don't, and we're not deficient for having a learning curve. Here are some phrases to use when you can't answer a question.

- What do *you* think?
- Let me check on that and get back to you.
- I don't know, but I'll find out.
- I'll research that and get back to you. What background information can you give me to inform my decision?
- I haven't learned that yet. Do you want me to find out for you, or do you have another place to get that information?
- In my previous position this is how we handled it. I don't know the procedure here yet. I'll find out.
- I'm going to wait for (item) to make a decision.
- I will let you know as soon as I have gathered enough information to decide.
- That information is confidential. What I can tell you is (more limited info). (Use this for truly confidential information. Don't hide behind it because you don't know the answer.)
- Because I could only provide a partial answer now, I'll wait to answer until I can give you a complete answer.

Perfect Phrases to Establish Yourself with Your Manager

Sometimes our own managers need a little nudge to support us in doing the jobs we were hired to do. Here are some phrases to elicit help.

- What advice do you have for me as a new manager?
- What assignments do you want me to take off your plate?
- I want to free your time up as much as possible. How do you see me doing that?
- I need my team to come to me directly in order to supervise effectively. Will you encourage them to do that?
- Can I count on you to refer my staff back to me when they come to you with a request they should direct toward me?
- I assume you want my team to report to me now instead of you. When do you want them to come directly to you?
- Am I free to make decisions about (item) without consulting you?
- I plan to send you a written weekly update to ensure information continuity. Does that work for you?

Perfect Phrases for Handling Employees Who Try to Take Over

Some employees confuse an invitation for collaborative input with abdication. When employees try to take over, here are some words you can use.

- I have a collaborative style and like to get everyone's perspective before I commit to a course of action. I'd like your input in my decision too.

- Sometimes employees confuse a request for input with a request for making my decision for me. Your input will expand my thinking, even if I don't seem to apply what you say.

- I understand you have strong ideas about how this should be done. I'll consider them before I make my decision. Your input is important, and this is my decision to make.

- Are you aware that you went over my head when you did that?

- I appreciate your expertise in this area. However, the success or failure of this project rests with me, and that is why I make the final decision about this.

- What prompted you to take that action without consulting me? (Careful with the tone on this one—be curious, not confrontational.)

- If you have problems with a decision, let me know. Otherwise, I assume you will be working as agreed.

- I made the decision to do it this way because (reason). Unless we come up with a better way that we both agree to, I need you to follow this procedure. Will you commit to that?

- You have great ideas and I want you on my team to come up with a better approach. Until then, everyone needs to do it this way, including you. Are you on board?

- Here are the situations where I want you to make the decisions (list). Here are the situations where the decision rests with me (list). This is because (reason). We can talk about it and adjust if there is a problem. Otherwise, please follow instructions.

Perfect Phrases to Introduce Hands-On Involvement

We need to familiarize ourselves with the jobs our employees do. Perfect Phrases gracefully let them know we plan to shadow them.

- I will shadow you in your work occasionally. It is not to check *up* on you; it is to check *in* with you.

- I understand you're used to working on your own. My goal is to learn what I can to help you do your job, to find out how I can support you.

- You're the expert because you do this every day. I want to learn from your expertise.

- The more I understand your job the better I will be able to support you.

- A manager once told me, "If you want to learn how to do a job, go to the people who do it." I'd like to learn from you.

- Sometimes a second pair of eyes catches things others miss. I'll be familiarizing myself with what you do, asking questions, learning from you, and providing a second pair of eyes.

Perfect Phrases to Announce Change Gracefully

Since many people don't like change, it's important to choose our words with care when we announce new policies and initiatives. Here are some phrases.

- I'm committed to telling you about decisions that affect you.

- I have some changes to announce. I'll start with what is changing, when, and why. Then I will tell you who it will affect and how much control we will have over what happens.

- This is different from how we have been operating. Let me explain why it will benefit us all.

- Now that you have heard this latest news, what are your thoughts and feelings about it?

- What do you understand the changes to be and how they will affect you?

- I shared what information I have. I'll do my best to get answers to the questions I can't answer yet.

- I am aware of the following rumors. I want to address them all.

- Please share with me any rumors that you hear so I can clarify the situation.

- Passing rumors instead of verifying them is a destructive form of gossip. Gossip doesn't serve our team, but clarifying rumors does. I will respond to all questions about rumors you've heard.

Perfect Phrases to Handle Resistance to Change

If we anticipate resistance to our change announcements, we can soften it by addressing the possibility of resistance before it happens.

- I am about to announce a change. It will take some getting used to. If your first reaction is to resist, please check the impulse and give this change the chance to succeed.

- Like any change, this one will probably feel awkward at first. Once you are used to it, I expect it will feel more natural than what we are doing now.

- It's human nature to try to resist change. My goal is not to defeat resistance. My goal is to help us all move through the resistance, accept this change, and become more productive as a result.

- I invite your suggestions to help us get through this transition and make it as easy as possible.

- Here are the problems we are experiencing. If we do not solve the problem ourselves, upper management will dictate changes. Let's make our own changes.

- I understand why some of you might resist this change. It's mandated and I need you all behind it. How can we all get behind this?

- When I first heard about this change, I had doubts, too. But now that I understand it better, I see how it's going to work. Let me explain.

Perfect Phrases to Support Change You Don't Agree With

If we disagree with a new initiative, we can express our opinions directly to our supervisors. When we announce unwelcome changes to our teams, we don't need to pretend to like them, but we do need to express full support of them.

- Management has decided to make this change and as part of the management team, I support it.

- I understand this change will create more work for you and isn't popular. Still, it's our policy now. I'm open to input about how we can smoothly implement it as long as we are supporting the initiative.

- This is what was decided and this is what we're going to do. We can move forward resentfully and make ourselves miserable or we can find a way to live with it. I say we make the best we can of it.

- I know this is difficult. Since we don't have a choice, let's talk about how we can make it work.

- We have four choices with this change. We can accept it as directed, adapt it to our situation, quit, or suffer. The last two aren't options most of us want to take.

Chapter 4

Perfect Phrases to Create a Mission, Vision, and Values-Based Team

People burn out more from a lack of purpose than from a lack of energy.[1] We can establish that purpose by inviting our employees to respond to the questions "Why are we here?" and "What are we trying to do?" with heartfelt answers they can commit to. If our teams have a shared vision of purpose, they will move in the same direction. If our teams have shared values, they can work together to get the job done. When we do a good job defining mission, vision, and values and engage our employees in the process, it establishes them in our team's minds and hearts. The mission, vision, and values will guide daily decisions and will foster commitment and involvement.

When I speak about mission and values in management seminars, many managers roll their eyes, groan, and slouch back in their chairs. That's because they work for companies that have mission statements in name only. Few are following the mission

---

[1]James M. Kouzes and Barry Z. Posner, *Leadership Challenge*. San Francisco: Jossey-Bass, 2007.

and many don't even know what the mission statement is. The mission was created without synergistic engagement.

I recently asked a new associate to help me refine my mission, vision, and values. She was deeply moved that I asked her to engage at that level, and she was quite emphatic about how that kind of engagement deepened her commitment.

That contrasts with one company where the executive committee spent countless hours developing the company values, goals, and mission. When they completed it, they posted it on every bulletin board. One of the primary values listed was respect: "We respect our clients, our vendors, and our co-workers." One of the executives that helped write the mission statement practiced management by intimidation. He yelled at his staff during meetings, sometimes yelled at clients, and was rude to vendors. Staff figured the executive would not be allowed to behave that way if upper management really valued what the statements said they did.

If you have a fixed organizational mission statement, reinforce it by applying it in things you say and do. In addition, work with your group to create a complementary statement for your own department or team. One caution: if you're not prepared to walk the talk, don't write it. You will do more harm than good.

If you are willing to manage by principles, use the following Perfect Phrases to help you draw out the common mission, vision, and values. Most of the phrases are in the form of a question so you can use them to brainstorm.

Perfect Phrases to Establish Mission

Our missions define the purpose of our teams, departments, and organizations. For example, the mission of my organization, SpeakStrong Inc., is "To work with individuals and leaders at every level who have moved beyond victimhood and power games and seek to liberate their thinking and communication from remaining vestiges of limitation and contention, and to empower magnetic influence based on confluent communication and reciprocal engagement."

That mission still makes me shiver.

If your organization has a mission statement, reinforce it. Instead of skipping this section, use it to create a department or team mission that makes you and your team shiver too. Ask some of the following questions:

- What would a perfect world look like where everyone benefited from what we do?

- Fill in the blank: Imagine a world where . . .

- If we could only accomplish one thing, what should it be?

- Why are we important?

- What makes us great?

- What makes us unique?

- What is our greatest contribution to the (world, customers, company)?

- What do our customers really want from us?

- If our customers wrote our mission statement, what would it say?
- What do you like about our company?
- What don't you like about our company?
- Considering the input, what would you say our mission is?
- How can we rank these missions?
- Which of these missions is the highest priority?
- Is this a mission you can believe in?
- What would make it more relevant for you?

Perfect Phrases to Establish Vision

Our visions are our pictures of possibilities for our organizations and units. For example, the vision of SpeakStrong is "To make the new dynamics of communication a communication standard. To become the leading experts on evolving communication trends. To model the new dynamics of communication in word and deed."

We may fall short of our vision, but we strive toward it.

Use these phrases to encourage your team to form a shared vision to strive toward.

- Here is my picture of what we can do. What pictures do you have?

- How do you see us at our best?

- If we could become whatever we wanted and we knew we could not fail, what would we look like?

- How do you picture us being as valuable to the larger organization as possible?

- Realistically, what can we envision?

- Where are you personally in that picture?

- If you could change anything, what would it be?

- How does your vision for yourself blend with your vision for the company?

- What are you willing to do to make this vision happen?

- Are you willing to commit to this vision?

- How would you rank the proposed visions?

- Which visions inspire you most?

Perfect Phrases to Establish Values

A value is a principle, standard, or quality considered worthwhile or desirable. For example, the SpeakStrong values are the new dynamics of communication. We strive to observe them in everything we do.

People prioritize work according to their values. If you have conflict, it could be the result of differing values. Most companies have stated values. If your company has stated values, keep them in mind for yourself and your team. Take it a step further and use these Perfect Phrases to determine team values.

- What values feed our mission and vision?
- What values do we share?
- What matters most: quality, service, or profit?
- What do you like about our products (services)?
- What would make you like our products (services) more?
- What do you like about how we operate?
- What would make you like how we operate more?
- What makes work worth doing for you?
- Name two people you admire and two qualities they each embody.
- What values would you be willing to die for?
- What does it mean to work here?
- What do you want it to mean?
- What qualities do you believe should drive our business?

- If we stop thinking about what we *should* value and review what we *do* value, what would we come up with?
- Which of these values are most important?
- What values are we willing to commit to?

Perfect Phrases to Empower the Mission, Vision, and Values

After we create our mission, vision, and values, Perfect Phrases dynamize them. No matter how well designed our vision, mission, and values are, they are worthless unless we apply them. Refer to yours routinely. Tie the most mundane activity into the bigger picture. Here are some phrases to help you do that.

- This initiative aligns with our mission because (reason).

- Your job requirement of (activity) may seem mundane, but it contributes to our mission in a significant way.

- It may seem like you're just (answering the phone, shuffling numbers, fighting little fires), but in fact you are contributing to our mission in an indispensible way.

- If we are serious about achieving our vision of (vision), this (project, idea, decision) will help us by (benefit).

- Since our top value is (value), I suggest we proceed by (action step).

- Which decision best fulfills our (mission, vision, values)?

- I admire your commitment to our (mission, vision, values).

- This milestone shows a deep commitment to our team (mission, vision, values).

- Let's use our (mission, vision, values) to decide this.

- If we are really committed to our values, we'll address this issue.

■ Remember why we're here.

■ This decision is not consistent with our mission.

■ Remember our mission.

It's worth the time to develop values. I see teams, departments, and companies that operate with a high degree of energy and alignment because they are committed to the same mission, vision, and values. Sometimes when they tell me what they stand for, I don't get it. But I don't need to. Your mission doesn't need to inspire me. It needs to inspire you.

I watched in awe as a group from a hotel chain stood up and sang their mission statement with pride and pleasure to a room of seminar attendees. They let their commitment show. Let yours show too. No, you don't have to put your statements to music, but it wouldn't hurt! If you and your team are guided by shared mission, vision, and values, your employees will make decisions in your absence that will be the same as decisions while you're there. And you will be well on your way toward a harmonious, synergistic engagement.

Chapter 5

Perfect Phrases to Foster Open Communication

ommunication is two-way by definition. So much of what managers call communication really isn't. Genuine communication happens when employees feel safe to speak freely. How often does that occur? Few employees report feeling safe questioning instructions and directives. That means bad ideas regularly go unchallenged and good ideas are often never heard. That means employees don't dare to say no to projects that overload them past capacity. That means employees hesitate to question unclear directions and make up what they don't understand. That means employees aren't really team members because the team isn't really a team. We can't afford to have that be our world.

Managers often discourage communication without realizing it. Do you ever ridicule an idea? Are you ever defensive when criticism is directed against you? Have you ever retaliated either directly or indirectly against someone who spoke up? If you have, you sent a message throughout the team that it is not safe to speak. When we help the people we supervise feel safe speaking up or asking questions, we benefit from their ideas, we can address minor problems before they become major issues, and we are less likely to be faced with unpleasant surprises.

The beauty of open communication is much greater than the problems it avoids. The beauty is in the possibilities it unfolds. Troubleshooting becomes a synergistic fiesta. Brainstorming becomes fervent. A routine meeting can energize the team enough to solve the energy crisis. (I exaggerate, but you get the point.) I recently returned from a synergistic meeting with my team so on fire with ideas that I got more work done in an hour than I had the previous week. (This time I'm not exaggerating.)

So let's not just use synergy to avoid problems. Let's use it to become vital and strong. The phrases below will help you get going.

Perfect Phrases to Ensure Employees Keep You in the Loop

- If you ever wonder if you should tell me something or cc me on something, go ahead and do it.

- Please tell me about any changes regarding (topic). I don't need you to tell me about (other topic).

- Is there anything going on I might want to know?

- I know you know how to do your job. Just update me to keep me in the loop.

- I want to check *in* with you, not check *up* on you.

- I'll tell you about anything that affects you. Please tell me about anything that affects me and the team.

- Please give me an update of your progress by (time).

- Is the project running on schedule?

- Is everything within budget?

- Are the quality specifications being met?

- What can I do to support your work?

- No one told me about (item). Next time, please update me about events like that.

- My manager said you came to him directly about (topic). I am concerned that you went over my head, but I'm more concerned about our relationship. What made you decide not to come to me first?

- If you include me earlier in the process, we can synergize our thinking and come up with ideas neither one of us could come up with alone.

Perfect Phrases to Encourage Feedback

Sometimes employees don't believe managers really do want feedback. They need extra permission and encouragement to offer an alternative perspective. They're so accustomed to looking for the "right" answer that they are afraid to give input. Here are some phrases to give extra encouragement.

- Imagine you *did* have an objection to this initiative. What would it be?

- Please tell me what you like about this plan (procedure, idea, etc.). What would make you like it more?

- What do you believe could conceivably go wrong with this in the worst possible scenario?

- What do you think of this? There is no right answer.

- Do you see a better way of doing this?

- What do (I, we, you) need to know to make this endeavor successful?

- What have I overlooked? Is there something that is outside my radar that would be useful?

- Pretend I don't know anything. What would you tell me about this? If we both have the same perspective on this, one of us is unnecessary.

- I didn't hire you to agree with me. Synergize with me, yes, but agree with me, no.

Perfect Phrases to Encourage Questions on Policies and Directives

- Please ask three questions about my task request. If we are making assumptions, I'd like to find out now.
- I want to make sure my instructions are clear. What is your understanding of what I just said?
- What did I leave out?
- What would you like reviewed?
- What will your first step be?
- What questions do you have?
- What ideas do you have about (topic)? I might be missing something.
- Please take a moment and summarize our discussion so far.
- What main points stand out in what we said?
- Let's see if I communicated well. What did you hear me say?
- I want to make sure we are headed in the same direction. Where do you plan to start?

Perfect Phrases to Get a Quiet Employee to Communicate

■ Some people on the team share everything and drown out the quieter ones. I want to hear more of what you have to say.

■ I used to hold back from talking to my manager because I didn't know if it was safe. I want you to feel safe talking to me. Please test me.

■ We need your input to move forward.

■ This is not personal. This affects our ability to do our jobs. Tell me where you stand on this.

■ I often find the team members who speak the least are the ones who have the most to say. What's on your mind?

■ How can I make it easy for you to share what you think about what's going on?

Perfect Phrases to Encourage Team Members to Communicate Directly and Effectively with Each Other

We waste a lot of time when team members go through us when they should be dealing directly with each other. Plus it can be divisive when we hear issues individually, from only one perspective. Here are some phrases to get employees talking to each other.

- Who do you think needs to know about changes regarding (topic)?
- Let's make a list of all the stakeholders in this project so you can update them about developments.
- What information do you need to update (Name) on?
- Have you spoken with (Name) about this?
- Please talk to (Name) directly about this.
- I'd like a joint recommendation.
- I notice you didn't copy (Name) on this e-mail. Please include (him, her) in future communications.
- I'd like for you to handle this directly with (Name).

Perfect Phrases to Encourage Employees to Admit Mistakes

If we react poorly when employees tell us about their mistakes, we're likely to create a dynamic where they don't tell us about problems until it's too late. Here are some phrases to encourage employees to admit their mistakes.

- I like to replace the word *mistakes* with "learning experiences." I've had plenty of those.

- The way I like to hear about mistakes is with a plan of action to keep from making that mistake again.

- I assume there will be mistakes. That's normal.

- Please tell me when you make a mistake so I can help us both do our jobs better. It might be that I haven't guided you well.

- I expect mistakes. When you make mistakes, it tells me you're thinking, you're making decisions, and you're taking risks.

- When you make mistakes, try to make new ones, or the same ones at a more sophisticated level. But even if you make the same old ones, do tell me.

Perfect Phrases to Encourage Employees to Resolve Conflict

When team members collide, our challenge is to keep from siding with one employee over another. However, we do want to avoid staying so neutral that an aggressive employee can tyrannize others. First get them talking.

- If you have an issue with (Name), please talk with (him, her) directly. If you need support with the issue, I can meet with you both. It's not fair to either of you for me to hear your perspective when (Name) is not here to share (his, hers).

- We can't afford to have team members who don't get along. I prefer you work it out yourself, but I am willing to help if you need me. I'm not willing to let this negative dynamic continue.

- I'm tasking you to come up with a way to work together. Let me know what you come up with by (time).

- You two don't have to like each other, but you do have to find a way to work together.

- Please describe the situation from the other person's perspective. What words would (she, he) choose?

Perfect Phrases to Invite Feedback About Your Performance as Manager

How open are you to feedback? Employees respect leaders who invite, listen to, and learn from the feedback they receive. These phrases and questions will help.

- I'd like feedback, and I don't want you to say what you think I want to hear. I do ask you to be gracefully assertive in your word choice, however.

- How does my communication style work for you? What works? What doesn't?

- How's my listening? Do you think I hear what you say?

- I know there are some things about how I (communicate, manage) that can be challenging. Is there anything specific that would help us work together?

- When I get focused, I may be (rude, abrasive, curt) without realizing it. If it's a problem for you, please tell me.

- When I improve as a manager, your job gets easier. That's why I need your feedback.

- This takes courage, but I'm going to ask the question anyway. What can I do better?

- I *am* interested in hearing what I'm doing right, but I'm particularly interested in what I could be doing better.

Chapter 6

Perfect Phrases to Ace the Interview You Conduct

B ad hires are costly. How can we know if the person sitting across from us is the answer to our prayer or our worst nightmare?

This chapter provides Perfect Phrases to successfully—and legally—learn what we need to know before we commit to the wrong person. We start by knowing what information we are looking for with every question we ask. We proceed by picking our words with care.

Perfect Interview Phrases for Gathering Personal Information

The phrases in this section are designed to determine if the candidate's situation and background are appropriate for the job, and to get the information we need without getting into legal trouble. Instead of asking age, citizenship, family situation, and health status, the Perfect Phrases below elicit the information we are really looking for: whether they can do the job we need them for.

- Do you have legal verification of your right to work in this country?

- What languages do you speak, read, or write?

- These are the hours, days, and shifts that you would be working. Is there anything that would interfere with your ability to work these hours?

- If we hire you, do you have proof of your age?

- Are you comfortable with our policy of not allowing personal phone calls at work?

- Is there anything that keeps you from being able to (task) with reasonable accommodation?

- This job requires lifting fifty pounds. Can you do that?

- Tell me about the most physically demanding job you have had.

- Tell me about the most volatile environment you've ever worked in.

Perfect Interview Phrases to Learn Work Styles and Preferences

These questions are designed to find out how candidates like to work.

- Do you prefer working alone or in groups?
- What personal style do you find it challenging to work with? Why?
- Do you like a lot of involvement or independence?
- What are some things you like to avoid in a job? Why?
- What is the most important thing you are looking for in a job?
- What were some of the things about your last job that you found challenging?
- What are some things you liked best about your last job?
- How do you feel about the way your last supervisor managed you?
- Why are you leaving your present job? (Or: Why did you leave your last job?)
- What is important to you in a company? What things do you look for in an organization?
- How much supervision are you used to?
- I see you worked at (place) from (date) to (date). Why did you choose that firm?
- What is the most important quality a person in this position should have?
- I'd like for you to interview me for the job of your manager. What do you need to know to see if this is a fit for you?

Perfect Interview Phrases to Learn Work Expectations

These questions are designed to uncover how candidates perceive the job they are applying for.

- What about the description of this job caught your interest?

- Where do you see yourself in five years?

- Tell me about your ideal job. How do you see this position compared to that ideal?

- Why are you applying for this position?

- How did you hear about this position?

- Is there anything you've had happen in previous jobs you're hoping won't happen here?

- If you get this job, what do you think would be the highlight of your day?

- If you get this job, what do you think would be your least favorite part?

Perfect Interview Phrases to Evaluate Interpersonal Skills

These questions uncover how candidates handle the kinds of interpersonal challenges they are likely to face. (See Chapter 9 for interview questions regarding diversity interpersonal skills.)

- Tell me about a time a customer was offensive or obnoxious and how you handled it.

- Describe a situation where you were tempted to or did lose your temper with a dissatisfied customer.

- Have you ever lost your temper with a customer or co-worker?

- Tell me about a time when you turned an angry customer around.

- Describe a situation where you went the extra mile to satisfy a tough customer.

- Describe a situation where you needed to refuse an unreasonable request from your manager.

- If your manager offended you, how would you handle it?

- What would you do if you were on a team that wasn't communicating well?

- How would you handle a co-worker who stole your idea?

- How do you respond to gossip?

Perfect Interview Phrases to Determine Self-Directedness, Personal Motivation, and Creativity

Self-directedness, personal motivation, and creativity are valuable assets in most situations. However, if we are interviewing for a routine job, we want to be sure the candidate won't feel stifled. We can find out about the directedness and creativity of our applicant with the Perfect Phrases below.

- What have you done that you consider truly creative?

- Can you think of a time when the way things were done didn't work too well and you found a new way?

- What kind of problems do people call on you to solve?

- How comfortable are you with repetitive tasks?

- Tell me about an obstacle you had to overcome and how you handled it.

- What have you done to prepare yourself to work in this field?

- How do you organize your time?

- What have you done in the past when you discovered a work area that needed improvement?

- What are some of the obstacles you found in previous jobs? How did you handle them?

- How do you keep up with what's going on in your (company, industry, profession)?

- How many nonfiction books did you read last year?

- How important is it to you to be the best?

Perfect Interview Phrases to Determine Leadership Qualities

These questions are designed to determine whether a candidate waits for others to guide or fills in leadership gaps where needed. They are also designed to determine whether a candidate considers the big picture or not.

- How do you get results from people you have no control over?

- Have you taken a leadership development course?

- How have you helped your (subordinates, co-workers) develop themselves?

- In your present job how do you get people to find a common approach to a problem?

- What do you do to get people to accept your ideas or department goals?

- Tell me some specific things you've done to set an example for others.

- Do people consider you a leader?

- How do you help people get along?

- If you were the president of this company, what is one new (policy, plan, product) you would initiate?

- How do you motivate people?

- Give an example of how you once saw a need and filled it.

- Do you see every employee as having a leadership role in an organization?

Perfect Interview Phrases to Determine Resourcefulness and Situational Qualifications

These questions address the candidate's approach to situations he or she is likely to experience and determine whether the candidate has relevant experience.

- How do you handle it when two managers insist you give their projects priority?

- If you had a crisis and needed an immediate decision from your manager and you couldn't reach him or her, what would you do?

- What's your experience with (skill)?

- What work experience prepared you for this job?

- How often do you use the Internet to solve problems?

- If a doctor gave you a diagnosis that didn't seem right, would you get a second opinion? What else would you do?

- I'll tell you about a situation the person who was previously in this position had to deal with. Then I'd like for you to tell me how you would have handled it.

- Have you ever found an opportunity through social media connections?

- Do you belong to professional organizations? Which ones? How have they helped you succeed? How have they helped your employer?

- What awards have you received for work performance?

- What would your previous (staff, co-workers, managers, team members) say about you?

Perfect Interview Phrases to Determine Education and Training

Not all relevant learning shows up on a standard interview form. These questions uncover formal training and also learning that may not fit into a standard job application.

- What formal or informal education or training has prepared you for this job?

- Have you advanced your knowledge and skills through online training? How?

- Have you had a formal or informal mentor who taught you things that would help you with this job?

- What else has provided you with knowledge useful for this job?

- What has been the most important person or event in your own self-development?

- What kind of books and other publications do you read?

- What skills do you have that are self-trained?

- How did you get that training?

- How much do you use the Internet to get ideas and solve work-related problems?

Perfect Interview Phrases to Determine Career Goals

Employees are more likely to be motivated if their career goals match the opportunities you offer. We can find out what those are with the questions listed below.

- What is your long-term employment or career objective?
- How do you see this job fitting into that objective?
- What skills and knowledge will you need to do that?
- Why do you believe you will be successful doing that?
- If you had this job, what would you like to accomplish?
- What might make you leave this job?
- What would cause you to stay for a long time?

Perfect Interview Phrases to Determine Work Standards

Some employees take ownership of projects and are committed to successful outcomes. Others are just doing a job, without the commitment to do what it takes to excel. Find out what your candidate's approach is.

- Can you give an example of a time you saw a need and filled it without being asked to?
- How do you measure success in your job?
- Do you expect to leave work exactly on time every day?
- How many sick days do you consider acceptable?
- Define what a good job is in your position.
- Define what a great job is in your position.
- How do you evaluate others' performance? What factors do you consider?
- Tell me about a project you were involved with that didn't go as well as you expected. Why did it fall short?
- Tell me about a project that went better than expected. Why was it so successful?

Perfect Interview Phrases to Determine Flexibility

Most jobs require flexibility. These Perfect Phrases determine if a candidate has the flexibility the position requires.

- What was the most important idea or suggestion you received recently? Did you change anything as a result?

- How do you handle constant changes in company operating policies and procedures?

- What was the most significant change made in a company you worked for? How successful were you in implementing that change?

- When you're in the middle of a project and your manager calls with an immediate request, how do you handle it?

- Have you ever had a manager change directions in the middle of a project? How did you respond?

- How do you handle it when a manager asks you to do things outside your job description?

Perfect Multipurpose Interview Sentence Stems

Open-ended questions elicit information better than closed ones. These sentence stems can help you assess even more about the candidate.

- What . . .
- Explain . . .
- Describe . . .
- How would you . . . ?
- In what ways . . . ?
- Under what circumstance do you . . . ?
- If you could . . . ?
- Please cite some examples of . . .
- Tell me about . . .

Chapter 7

Perfect Phrases for Employee Orientation

As the old proverb says, "Well begun is half-done." While we're at it, let's also recall the proverb "a stitch in time saves nine." It's worth our time to start employees out right. Too often orientation means showing new hires their work space and running off to fight a fire or resolve a crisis. Since we never get a second chance at a first impression, we need our Perfect Phrases to help our new employees feel welcome and oriented.

Perfect Orientation Phrases to Greet and Welcome

- We are glad you are here because . . .

- We are looking forward to having someone here with your experience in . . .

- Let me introduce you. This is (Name) and (he, she) is responsible for . . .

- We know what it's like to be new, and we're here to help the transition go smoothly.

- We have the following measures to help you through the inevitable learning curve.

- When you get stuck, here's what you do.

- When you need help, this is whom you turn to.

- If we get caught up in our own activities and forget to anticipate what you will need, let us know.

- What questions do you have now?

Perfect Orientation Phrases to Introduce the New Employee to the Company

- The history, mission, and goals of the (department, company, organization) are . . . Here's where you can get more information on them.

- Let me show you the organizational chart. If you direct a communication to the wrong person, we'll redirect you.

- The employee handbook actually is a great source of information for you. Please review it and bring me your questions. Then we can highlight what we see as the most relevant policies.

- Here is the operating manual from the person who had the job before you. I expect it will be useful, and I also know you will develop your own approaches.

- Security information and your ID card are available at the . . .

- Benefits information is available through . . .

- If you have any safety concerns or injuries contact . . .

- The parking info you need is . . .

Perfect Orientation Phrases to Reinforce Disciplinary Policies

Some of these phrases address information that should be in the company manual. When we verbalize them, we reinforce them, and the policies find their way into our employee's awareness.

- We require our employees to dress according to the following dress code. (Code.)

- Our absenteeism policy is (detail).

- As our manual states, employment here is at will. That means either one of us can end your employment at any time.

- If you ever need to file a grievance, this manual tells you how. I can help, unless the grievance is with me, of course. I'm planning on that not happening, but if it should, contact . . .

- Our policy about proprietary information is . . .

- Other key policies that all employees need to know before starting their jobs are . . .

Perfect Orientation Phrases to Get New Employees Started

- Please start by attending to the . . . If you need me, the best time and the best way to reach me is . . .

- Your job responsibilities are . . . We will meet to clarify them on (date), and we can see if they need to be adjusted.

- Please review your position description so we can discuss expectations and standards.

- Your workdays and hours are . . . Is that what you expected?

- Your position description provides the framework and essential job duties for your scope of responsibility.

- The position description provides clarity on priorities and helps you understand how you will be evaluated.

Perfect Orientation Phrases to Establish Feedback

- Plan to meet with me (weekly, daily, twice weekly, etc.) for the first six months.

- Regular meetings provide an opportunity to clear up misunderstandings, clarify priorities, and develop a synergistic working relationship.

- So I can coordinate and oversee you and so you can do your job, we need to be completely honest with each other about how things are going.

- My goal is to empower you to handle issues on your own as soon as possible. In the beginning you can expect me to be very involved. That will decrease as you learn the ropes.

- Initially, if you have any questions about (item), bring them to me and let me decide.

- Initially, if you have any questions about (item), bring them to me and we'll decide how to handle it.

- If you have any questions about (item), decide what to do and let me know what you decided.

- Decide about (item) on your own. Don't worry about telling me about it unless you want to.

- You are free to make decisions about (item) without consulting me.

- If you have any issues that require immediate attention, here's how you can get hold of me.

- I prefer to hear from team members during (times). If something needs immediate attention, contact me immediately.

Perfect Orientation Phrases to Introduce the New Employee to the Culture

- Office etiquette around here is to (return calls within three hours, clean the coffeepot when less than one cup remains, etc.).

- The way people socialize around here is (lunch, birthday parties, social activities, etc.).

- Generally the culture is (casual, formal, driven, competitive, cooperative, etc.).

- Always copy (Name) on anything related to (item).

- The standard format for letters and memos is (format).

- A great way to build relationships between colleagues, supervisor, and staff is to (method).

- Our company has a (softball, bowling, racquetball, etc.) team. All employees are welcome to participate. If you're interested, talk to (Name).

Chapter 8

Perfect Phrases for Netiquette, Social Media, and Other Online Activities

Because Internet use and social media are relatively new, there is no standard about how to use them. That's why I have singled these topics out for discussion. We need clear guidelines and shared understanding of what is appropriate and acceptable in the new online world that we officially and unofficially live in. These phrases back up an existing online policy. If you don't have one, please create one.

Perfect Phrases to Discuss E-Mail Use

- I consider twenty-four hours an appropriate response time for routine e-mails. Does that work for you?

- When there is some kind of conflict or opportunity for misunderstanding, instead of e-mailing me, please call.

- I notice you don't have a signature code on your e-mail. A signature code would make it easier for clients to reach you. Do you know how to add one?

- I received a nonbusiness forward from you. Did you know our e-mail policy prohibits that?

- Are you aware that e-mails sent on company computers are considered company property?

- Please keep private any messages sent to you unless I or other senders OK passing them on.

- To streamline our communication, I'd like our team to create and apply e-mail shortcuts such as EOM, meaning "end of message," and NRN, meaning "no response necessary." What suggestions do you have?

- When an e-mail extends below the fold, it's time to create a separate one or to pick up the phone and talk.

- Please update subject lines in our e-mails for easier searching.

- This e-mail was so long I decided it was time to call.

Perfect Phrases to Discuss Texting and Tweeting

■ Texting divides your attention, and our policy calls for you to limit messaging to company-related messages.

■ Texting is a useful tool, and we have a lenient texting policy to allow you to use it. However, if it seems like texting costs rather than enhances productivity, we will have to adjust our policies to limit its use. I don't want that to happen, so please help us keep things more on the honor system.

■ Are you aware that texting on company phones is prohibited while driving? It is cause for immediate dismissal.

■ It distracts from everyone when someone at a meeting isn't giving his or her full attention. If you're texting or tweeting during a meeting, it might mean you don't belong at the meeting. If that's true, we can talk about it. If you are at a meeting, please give it your full attention.

■ Last month many of you were on Twitter while the CEO spoke to us at the conference. Are you aware that we know you do that—that social media is visible?

Perfect Phrases to Discuss Social Media Policy

- We (encourage, discourage) you as our employees to get involved in social media.

- If you use our name in your social media posts, please use your own name too.

- What you publish online will be around for a long time, and you never know how someone might use it, so be careful about disclosing personal details.

- I saw your post about your promotion on Facebook. I'm delighted for your success. I did notice your post contained some proprietary information. Please take down the part about (topic).

- I notice you've been blogging during work hours. How does that enhance our mission?

- If you want to use social media at work, please develop a system so it doesn't interfere with your responsibilities.

- Did you know that more than half of hiring mangers Google their candidates these days? Social media can carry more weight than a résumé.

Perfect Phrases to Discuss Your Social Media Relationships with Employees

One of my employees made a friend request to me on Facebook, which I accepted. Then I asked another if she wanted to be part of my network and she agreed. Not all the people I've worked with have wanted to do so, however. We don't want employees to feel any pressure to include us in their networks. Here are some phrases you may want to use when discussing (or beginning) social media relationships with employees.

- I want to invite you to be part of my network, but I don't want to put you on the spot of having to decline. Would you prefer to keep your network more personal, or would you welcome a request?

- I didn't add you to my network to spy on you, but I did notice (questionable post). That makes me wonder about (issue), and it also makes me wonder if you are aware that I read these things.

- I'm noticing your social media posts are more personal than professional. Would you prefer I not be part of your network? You can "unfriend" me if you like.

- My network is more personal, so while I appreciate friend requests from work associates, I'll decline so I can keep the relationships separate.

Chapter 9

Perfect Phrases to Address Diversity

I nclusion is a touchy topic. We ignore it at our own peril. Diversity challenges can be about embracing protected classes that have a history of exclusion such as the disabled, blacks, and women. But they also could be about embracing an extravert in an office of introverts, a Caucasian in an office of Asians, or a man in an office of women. I face an inclusion challenge when I speak to special groups like the Better Hearing Colorado Association when I am the only person without a hearing disability. I address the situation so those who might judge me for things I don't know become conscious of their own prejudices. That way we can overcome them. These Perfect Phrases for diversity shine the light of day on the elephant in the living room—on the differences that make up diversity. Then we can overcome prejudices in our offices.

Perfect Phrases to Address Diversity During the Interview

- How has your experience and background prepared you for a workplace that actively promotes diversity?

- What is most challenging about working in a diverse environment? How do you handle that?

- What kinds of experiences have you had working with others with different backgrounds from yours?

- Have you ever had to adapt your work style to meet a diversity need or challenge? Tell me about it.

- How have you handled a situation when a colleague resisted diversity?

- What have you done to learn about diversity? How has that changed your way of relating?

- What strategies have you used to address diversity challenges? What worked? What didn't work?

- What advantages do you see with a diverse workplace?

Perfect Phrases to Address Diversity with a New Employee

- You add to the diversity here. I'd like to address that when I introduce you. Are you comfortable with that?

- When I talk about the diversity you bring to our team, is there anything you'd like me to say? Are there things you'd like me to avoid?

- Since I don't have your experiences, I might say things that don't come across as I intend. I invite you to give me feedback and educate me on assumptions I make or ways I misspeak. Are you willing to do that?

- I'm open to hearing any thoughts—even negative thoughts—about our diversity policy. We need to talk about these issues and bring them into the open so we can solve them and move on to what's important: doing the best work we can.

- I don't want us to be tiptoeing around political correctness with each other, and I don't want us to be inadvertently offending each other either. When someone says or does something that expresses a cultural prejudice against you, please educate the team member instead of reacting. Teach us how you want us to treat you.

Perfect Phrases to Introduce a Diverse New Employee to the Team

- I'm excited to welcome (Name) to our team. We will all benefit from (Name's) experience and perspectives.

- Please welcome (Name) to our team. As you can see, (he, she) will increase our diversity. This is an opportunity for us to learn about different experiences and perspectives.

- This company believes that diversity strengthens us as a company and as a team. We are happy to welcome (Name) to our team and look forward to the new perspectives we will enjoy.

- Now that our team includes people with different life experiences and backgrounds, I don't expect us to ignore the ways we're different. I do expect us to discuss similarities and differences in a spirit of seeking understanding without aggression or defensiveness.

- As I look around the room, I see many cultures and races. I am grateful for this diversity because your various backgrounds and ways of thinking help us solve problems.

- We all have different life experiences, although some of those differences are greater than others. I expect there will be some inadvertent instances where negative feelings are triggered. When that happens, I also expect we'll use those as learning opportunities.

Perfect Phrases to Address Diversity Issues

Diversity issues indicate the need to work some alchemy and get all parts working in harmony. Here are some phrases to help you accomplish that.

- I've heard rumors about the team not accepting our new employee. I'd like to get the situation out in the open where we can deal with it.

- How are we doing welcoming our new team member? What are we doing right? How can we improve?

- I believe the issue you're having with (Name) might be a result of cultural differences. It's easy to judge others' norms, but it's useful to take a look at the cultural differences that are behind them.

- I can imagine why (remark, behavior) is offensive to you. Since I don't have the history of exclusion that you do, I can't know how deeply wounding it is to be treated that way. That said, I believe we can move forward if we use this incident as a learning opportunity for all of us. Please teach us how you want us to treat you.

- As you know, we have a nondiscrimination policy. What have you seen or heard that I need to know about?

- I've heard that you have been critical of (Name)'s work, saying that wasn't a job for someone of that (race, gender, etc.). Are these stories true?

- According to the law and our company manual, discrimination is prohibited. Please come to my office and talk any time something bothers you.

- We all have prejudices. We need to set those feelings aside while we're here. We expect everyone to treat each other fairly and courteously regardless of race, religion, color, disability, gender, or sexual preference.

- I have heard of some discriminating behavior. I don't expect you to talk about it in a public forum, but I want you to know I'm paying attention and will address it privately. I want to get to the root of culturally based conflict and move forward.

- I will not tolerate discrimination in any form. I will document anything I witness or hear from others. But I also will do whatever I can to move us past judgment to discernment.

- That type of activity excludes some of the cultures and abilities here, so we need to find an alternative that is inclusive.

Chapter 10

Perfect Phrases for Delegation

Delegation—getting work done through others—is one of the most underused tools of managers. Good delegation involves phrases that are clear, complete, accepted, and understood.

Perfect Phrases to Encourage Buy-In

Sure, it may be their job, but if employees are motivated, they will do their job much better than if they are not. Use the phrases below to encourage them to do their best—not because they have to, but because they want to.

- There is an opportunity here for you to . . .

- This project needs to be done right. That's why I'm bringing it to you.

- I'm asking you to do this because I know I can trust you.

- I know how busy you are. However, I have a request.

- I have a project I can only trust my very best (rep, manager, engineer) with.

- I need your help.

- I have a project that is outside your usual area that I think you will enjoy.

- What this project means to you is . . .

- This project will help you by (benefit), and it will also help the team by (benefit).

- I'll make sure my manager knows you made a difference when I really needed you.

Perfect Phrases for Clear Delegation

Here are some items to include when delegating. Clarity up front saves time and error.

- I need (item) by (date) because . . .

- I have written out instructions. Let's go over them together.

- The deadline is (date), the quality specifications are (specs), and the budget is (budget).

- Of these three, the priority in this project is (priority).

- An example of what it will look like is (example).

Perfect Phrases to Ensure Understanding of an Assignment

Once we explain a task, it's helpful to make sure our employees' understanding matches ours. Use Perfect Phrases to confirm.

- What questions do you have off the bat?
- What did I leave out?
- What would you like reviewed?
- What will your first step be?
- Let me make sure my instructions are clear. What is your understanding of what I told you?
- What questions remain?
- What ideas do you have about (aspect of job)?
- If you were required to question this assignment, what questions would you have?

Perfect Phrases to Elicit Input When You Delegate

Some employees hesitate to tell us if they find our directives confusing, our ideas ill advised, or their workload too heavy to take on a new task. Use Perfect Phrases to elicit input.

- Do you see a better way of doing this?

- What do you see as a challenge here?

- Does this work for you?

- Will your current workload let you complete this on time?

- Please ask me a few questions about this assignment.

- When will you have that for me?

- Please update me on how this is going by the end of the week.

- Is there anything that might interfere with getting this done?

- What do you need from me to be able to complete this?

- This project takes priority. Let me know if something else will need to slide to complete this.

Perfect Phrases to Eliminate Reverse Delegation

Even if you've never heard of reverse delegation, chances are you've experienced it. It's when we delegate a project and somehow it ends up back on our own desk. Use these Perfect Phrases when an employee attempts to pass the assignment back to you.

■ I'll coach you through, but I won't do this for you. What do we need to go over?

■ What have you tried so far?

■ What have you considered that you haven't tried?

■ What can I do to help you complete this on your own?

■ If you're having trouble completing this, I probably haven't been as clear as I need to be. I gave this to you because (reason), and I want to keep it in your court as much as possible. So let's see what I can do to support your doing this yourself.

■ If you need training to complete this on your own, figure out what training you need and let me know if you need my support in getting it.

■ This is a learning experience I want you to have so you can master these skills. I am willing to invest the time in having you learn how to complete this project on your own.

Perfect Phrases to Refuse an Employee Request

How comfortable are you saying no? Most people aren't very comfortable and that shows up either as overly apologetic or overly harsh language. These phrases will help you decline requests in a gracefully assertive way.

- I'd like to say yes, but I can't because (reason). Here is what I *can* do for you.

- It's a great idea that I can't approve because . . .

- I know (request) is important to you. I can't approve it because . . .

- I can't say yes to that right now, but we can review the situation and see what you can do that would let me approve that in the future.

- What a great idea! I can't do that, but wish I could.

- No, but thanks for asking.

Perfect Phrases to Credential Employees

Sometimes team members need our credentialing to get the job done. Perfect Phrases help delegates get the cooperation they need to be effective.

- When (Name) asks for something, I expect you to give it to (her, him).

- (Name) is in charge of (project). Please give (him, her) your full cooperation.

- (Name) speaks for me.

- (Name) is working on an important project for me. Please give (his, her) requests the same priority you give mine.

- (Name) is taking over this project and has the authority to make decisions. Please refer questions to (her, him).

- I have given (Name) the authority to run this project as (he, she) deems appropriate.

- If (Name) asks you for help on this project, please make it your priority.

- When (Name) opens (her, his) mouth, my voice comes out.

Perfect Phrases for Follow-Up on Delegated Projects

If your employees struggle with a project or get behind schedule, they may try to cover their behinds rather than be up front. Minimize unpleasant surprises by scheduling follow-up meetings or putting follow-up on the agenda of previously scheduled meetings.

- Be prepared to update me on this in our weekly meeting.
- Let's check in (date) to see how this is going. If you have questions before then, let me know.
- Please update me on quality, budget, and deadlines.
- What can I do to support your work?
- Is there anything that might interfere with your successful completion of this project?
- Are you getting the cooperation you need?
- Do you need help to complete this on time?
- Are things working out the way we thought they would?

Chapter 11

Perfect Phrases to Set and Communicate Standards and Goals

Because this book focuses on verbal communication, the phrases here are for conversations about job standards and goals rather than for creating written standards and goals. I do include a sampling of actual job standards and performance goals so you can see what effective standards and goals are like. For a more complete list of potential job standards and performance goals, refer to *Perfect Phrases for Setting Performance Goals* by Douglas Max and Robert Bacal.

The way we communicate standards and goals can make the difference between standards and goals that guide the day-to-day operations, and standards and goals that are quickly forgotten.

Perfect Phrases to Set Job Standards

Job standards describe what we want any employee in that position to do. They are not individualized. They focus on what the employee *does*, not what the employee *is*. Great standards are concrete and come in two categories: behavioral and performance. Behavioral standards detail what employees do, and performance standards detail outcome.

Behavioral Job Standards Examples

- Make one personal comment to each customer per transaction.

- Develop and prepare forms, records, and charts to achieve effective workloads and workflow.

- Greet visitors, answer phone and take messages, and open and sort the director's mail.

- Monitor social media for company mentions. Alert managers of opportunities and issues.

- Come up with three questions for every assignment to make sure instructions are clear.

Performance Job Standards Examples

These examples refer to the result that the behavioral standards above are intended to create.

- Maintain existing customer service rating.

- Increase workflow by 30 percent.

- Keep the director focused on priorities.

- Increase social media mentions by 20 percent.

- Eliminate confusion on directives.

Perfect Phrases to Gather Input to Identify Job Standards

Employees shouldn't need to guess what their job is. In a synergistic environment, team members do help create their job descriptions, but they don't make their jobs up on their own. And they shouldn't find out what their jobs are at the performance review.

Today's workplace moves with so much momentum that standards and goals can be obsolete almost as soon as you set them. Instead of throwing up your hands in surrender, update and refine them continually.

Don't let previous descriptions limit you. My informal surveys indicate that while about 50 percent of employees have job descriptions, 80 percent of those descriptions do not come close to describing what the employee actually does. To make job standards relevant, use Perfect Phrases to investigate what the job really involves. Use these questions with the employees who already work in the position, employees who previously held the position, and co-workers who depend on and interact with the person in the position.

Perfect Questions to Ask Those Currently or Previously in the Position

Use these questions with those currently in the position or past position holders to get a clear picture of what the job involves.

- What (do you, did you) actually do every day?
- What is the main purpose of the job as you see it?

- What are the main responsibilities?

- What (do you, did you) do in this position that would have serious consequences if it didn't get done?

- What parts of the job aren't essential but are useful?

- Are there items in the job standards that you don't think are necessary anymore?

- What do others depend on this position for?

- What part of this job affects the mission and vision of the company? How?

- Is there anything you do that you're proud of that isn't reflected in these standards?

- Is there anything you do that is essential that isn't reflected in these standards?

Perfect Questions to Ask Those Who Depend on the Position

People who depend on the position are excellent information resources for what the job description should look like.

- What do you depend on the person in this position for?

- What do you see as essential for this position?

- What qualities and behaviors do you appreciate most from the person in this position?

- What job standards would you like to see the person in this position have?

■ Have you ever had to deal with problems that resulted from the person in this position not doing his or her job? What?

■ Are there any responsibilities that you have taken on that you think would more reasonably belong to this position?

Perfect Phrases to Confirm Agreement to Job Standards

Employees sometimes agree to standards without giving them much thought. Use Perfect Phrases to ensure job standards and affirm commitment.

- Do these standards make sense to you?

- These standards are solid expectations, not suggestions of what it would be nice for you to do. Is there anything about these standards that you do not feel able to commit to?

- Is there any way that you believe these standards need to be changed to make them more viable?

- Do you believe these standards define the essence of the job?

- Can you see how important to the company, team mission, and vision it is to fulfill these standards?

- Are you committed to these standards?

- How (will you, do you) show your commitment to these standards?

- Our formal review is set for (date). Don't wait until then to raise questions about the standards. And things change, so let me know if we need to adapt them.

Perfect Phrases to Reinforce Job Standards

Sometimes we set standards, and then we and everyone else promptly forget them. That's why we want to consistently reinforce standards. Standards will be the focus of performance reviews, but it's helpful for us to reinforce them between reviews.

- Let's look at what happened in light of your job standards.

- Is there confusion about the standards? Is your job clear to you?

- I notice (observation). Let's go over the standards and see what we need to change in how you do your job.

- I'm not asking for something arbitrary. It is part of the basic standards for this position.

- This function is standard for the job.

- If there are demands on your time that interfere with your meeting these standards, we need to correct that. The standards are the priority over all else.

Perfect Phrases to Negotiate Performance Goals

Performance goals are different from job standards. While anyone in a position is expected to meet standards, performance goals are specific to the individual and based on his or her strengths and weaknesses. Goals create focus, inspiration, and motivation. Goals that we negotiate with our team are the most dynamic.

- Now that we have the standards outlined, let's create goals for you to aspire to.

- The purpose of this meeting is for us to establish performance goals to give you focus, inspiration, and motivation.

- The best goals are ones we collaborate on.

- Where do you see room to do your job better than the standards call for?

- Although your job standards in this area are (detail the standard), I believe you are capable of more. Do you agree?

- What strengths would you like to develop?

- What specifically can you do to enhance those skills?

- I recommend you improve those skills by . . .

- How would improving those skills directly enhance your job?

- How would it benefit the company for you to target a higher standard in that area?

- How will we measure success?

- This goal is set to be achieved by . . .
- Our next formal review is set for (date). If you have any questions, want to brainstorm ways to reach the goals, or need to realign the goals before then, let me know.

Perfect Phrases to Set Behavioral and Performance Goals

Like job standards, performance goals also come in two categories: behavioral goals and performance goals. Here are some examples.

Behavioral Goals Examples

- Smile at customers at least twice per contact.
- Repeat back what a customer says at least five times per day.
- Read two books about the cultures represented here.
- Study your software tutorials.
- Attend college classes.

Performance Goals Examples

- Win the employee of the month award one month.
- Enhance your listening skills.
- Develop your relationships to other cultures.
- Become the most knowledgeable person on our team about spreadsheets.
- Get an advanced degree.

Perfect Phrases to Ensure Agreement to Performance Goals

As with job standards, employees sometimes agree to goals without giving them much thought. At times they will set themselves up for failure by being too ambitious. Other times they will commit to goals without taking them seriously. Perfect Phrases confirm performance goals and affirm commitment.

- Do these performance goals make sense to you?
- Is there anything about these performance goals that you can't commit to?
- Is there any way you think these performance goals need to be changed to make them more viable?
- Do you believe these performance goals are relevant to the essence of the job?
- Can you see how fulfilling these performance goals is important to the company, team mission, and vision?
- Are you committed to these performance goals?
- Will you put your commitment to these goals in writing?

Chapter 12

Perfect Phrases to Coach Employees

D o you mentor your team? Coaching is an important aspect of management. Coaching isn't just for a disciplinary role. Coaching our best employees to develop their potential is a good use of our time. Gallup research confirms that employees are happiest when their managers take a personal interest in them and their skills are put to good use. Perfect Phrases help.

Perfect Phrases for Informal Interaction

Don't limit feedback to the performance review. If you use MBWA (management by walking around), you'll create a presence in the workplace, and it will give you the chance for casual feedback.

- Hey, I like the way you (observation).
- By the way, great job on (item).
- I don't know how you do that, but I'm sure glad you do!
- Are you getting the help you need?
- Is there anything you need from me?
- How comfortable is your workload?
- Is there anything you want me to know?
- How was your weekend?
- What's your priority today?

Perfect Phrases to Uncover Employee Strengths

Gallup polls show that the best managers build on the areas where their employees are already strong. I find my team gets far more done when I align their projects with their interests. The following two sets of phrases uncover and build strengths.

- What part of your job is most exciting to you?

- Do you have freedom to perform this part of your job your own way?

- Does the amount of freedom you have contribute to your motivation and satisfaction with this part of your job?

- What would your perfect job look like?

- What could we do to make your job more like that?

- Are there some skills you would like to be able to use more and interests you'd like to be able to pursue?

- Can you think of something we should be doing that would draw on your skills?

Perfect Phrases to Build Employee Strengths

- I notice you have a knack for (skill). Are there some aspects of that skill you would like to develop?

- What would it take to develop that?

- How can I support you in getting even stronger in that skill?

- What do you like to do the most?

- What would you like to learn most?

- I'd like to give you further training in . . .

- I've got a job that has your name on it; I want to build your skills in the area of . . .

Perfect Phrases for Positive Reinforcement

Most employees never hear about it when they do something well. It's worth our time to tell our team what we appreciate about their work. Every phrase here calls for specific details about what is being acknowledged.

- (Project) was a very helpful initiative because . . .

- What made that a great job is . . .

- You just took us one step closer to our mission and vision.

- Way to go on that project.

- What makes this exceptional work is . . .

- I am particularly impressed by (action) because . . .

- What makes you great to work with is . . .

- I can tell you have an excellent sense of (quality) by . . .

- I appreciate how you consistently go out of your way to . . .

- Your professionalism shines in the way you . . .

- It's clear you put a lot of time and thought into . . .

- I know it was tough to (achievement), but you did it!

- Your results show your hard work.

- I noticed that you made significant changes in this report. It is more succinct and easier to understand, and the conclusions are clear.

- I can see that you worked hard to streamline this process. Your efforts have cut turnaround time in half. Thank you.

- When you did (action), it made my job easier because . . .

Perfect Phrases to Uncover and Address Issues and Obstacles

If performance is not up to standards, we need to avoid jumping to judgments about our employees' failures. Sometimes employees are not succeeding because they lack the skills. Sometimes employees are not succeeding because they don't know there's a problem. Sometimes employees are not succeeding because the system has built-in obstacles. Use these Perfect Phrases to address issues and uncover obstacles.

- I am generally pleased with your performance, especially (strong area). There is one thing I see a need to work on.

- Your job calls for you to (job standard), but what is happening instead is . . .

- Are there obstacles in the workplace that make it difficult for you to do your (job, project) well?

- Are there resources you need that you aren't getting?

- Do you have the resources to do this task?

- Do you understand the job standards?

- Are there skills you need to learn to do these tasks?

- Do you have enough authority to do these tasks?

- Are you getting the cooperation you need?

- Tell me what you think is happening.

- What would you say if I said I think you are an exceptional employee in the wrong position?

- I notice your performance hasn't been up to standards and I wonder if you're planning to leave the company. Are you?

Perfect Phrases to Brainstorm Solutions

When there is a performance problem, instead of dictating solutions, we're better off brainstorming them. These phrases get us started.

- This isn't working. I could just decide what to do about it, but I prefer we work together to solve the problem.

- Let's start by identifying the source of the problem. What do you think it is?

- Let's start by listing obstacles and see which ones we can change and which ones we'll need to work around.

- Let's brainstorm twenty possible ways to resolve this to get our creative juices flowing around the issue. The ideas don't have to be good—we'll evaluate them when we're done. I'll start.

- We need to fix this. I'd like to view it as an opportunity for us to move forward and move you to the next level.

- What would you do if you were me managing you in this situation?

- How committed are you to getting this right?

Perfect Phrases to Address Personal Issues and Counsel Grieving Employees

Personal issues and loss can affect performance. It's not our place to act like a therapist, but it is appropriate to empathize and direct the employee to services that can help. It is also our responsibility to address the workload, even in troubled times.

- You don't seem like your usual chipper self lately. Is something up?

- I understand wanting to keep your personal feelings private. If there is anything I can do to help, let me know.

- If you ever need to talk, I'm here.

- We do need to discuss your work performance. I don't know why your performance has dropped, and the job does need to get done.

- Your personal life isn't my business, and I'm not going to pry. It is affecting your work, and that is my business. So please know that I care, even though we do need to talk about your work.

- I encourage you to contact our EAP program for whatever support you can use. In the meantime, I need to know what I can count on with your job requirements.

- (Name), I am so sorry about your loss.

- It has to be hard dealing with loss.

- I am aware that you are under a lot of pressure. Let me know what I can do to support you.

- We don't expect you to be "up" all the time. Please feel safe to be real.

- I know I can't fix it, but I can listen.

- If we need to adjust your goals for a while, let me know.

- Obviously we need the job to get done, but let's see how we can adapt your requirements to accommodate your needs for a while.

- I find support groups to be incredibly helpful. I found one for your situation. Can I tell you about it?

Chapter 13

Perfect Phrases to Handle Performance and Behavior Problems

Many managers avoid problems until they can't anymore. Some wait until the performance review to address issues. Others even continue to ignore problems *at* the performance review. The best time for us to address a problem is when it begins.

Perfect Phrases for Real-Time Corrective Verbal Feedback

Here is some on-the-spot corrective feedback.

- What you did breaks the rules about (dress, attendance, safety, etc.). Are you aware of that?

- (Name), (action) is unacceptable because (reason).

- Thanks for the report. Are you aware that it was due this morning? It throws us all behind when we get it late. Next time, please (get it in on time, give us a warning when you know it's running late, ask for help getting the info you need for it, etc.).

- Are you aware of the effect of what you just did? (Explain.)

- Whether we like it or not, company policy states (policy). You have (action).

- How do you interpret the policy about (item)? When you (behavior) it violates that policy.

- Are you aware of the rules regarding (behavior)?

- Is there any confusion about what the standards are?

- The standards are (policy). What you did is (action). The impact is (result).

- I'm looking forward to the performance review. I want to be able to give you a great one. For that to happen I need for you to . . .

- Perhaps you intended that remark to be innocent. Let me tell you how it affected the team.

- When you said (comment), I noticed the team cringe. Let's look at how you can express yourself in a different way in the future.

- You are usually very punctual, but lately this is slipping. What's going on?

- I'm concerned about how (behavior) causes your team to perceive you. I'm afraid it will interfere with your job.

- We seem to be working at cross-purposes rather than together. What can we do to change that?

Perfect Phrases to Turn Informal Feedback into Verbal Warnings

The verbal warning is the first step of the disciplinary ladder. It can mark a shift in the relationship since we're giving our employees notice of the consequences to their actions. That can move the interpersonal dynamic from collaborative to a parental or adversarial one if we're not careful. It can show up in subtle ways such as moving from calling people "team members" to calling them "workers" or "staff." Watch your language for distinctions.

If you intend your feedback to serve as a warning for the record, say so. Inform employees of their status and possible consequences of their actions, but do it in a gracefully assertive way, without being threatening. It's a subtle but important distinction. Informing people is not the same as threatening them. These phrases help avoid sounding excessively heavy-handed.

- I am making a note of this discussion.

- I will note this as the first time we have discussed this.

- To be fair to you, I need to let you know that this is a verbal warning.

- I will document this conversation. That's the first step in the disciplinary procedure. I hope we can solve this issue without any further steps down the road.

- This is your first verbal warning. As you know from the handbook, you can receive (number of warnings) before termination is considered.

Perfect Phrases for Written Warnings and Counseling Sessions

Our next step on the disciplinary ladder is written warnings. We accompany written warnings with counseling sessions. Whatever we do in this process can have two audiences: the employee and a potential jury.

It's tough to avoid sounding parental at this point because most of the language in the process is parental. Plus, frankly, many employees get to the disciplinary process by acting like children. It's also difficult to avoid sounding heavy-handed because at this point we do need to use stronger words. A Perfect Phrase is as strong as it needs to be and no stronger. Assume an attitude of a supporter who is neutrally administering a procedure and wants to help the employee turn things around.

- I need to talk to you about your work progress. Please meet me in my office at (time).

- I'm worried about your continued (attendance problems, poor performance, demeanor with the team, etc.). It's reached the point of requiring a written warning. I have it for you to review. You may file a response.

- This is a written warning of poor performance and is part of the disciplinary process.

- This constitutes a formal written warning to you regarding . . .

- We will meet (day) at (time) to discuss this warning.

- You have the right to write a response to this warning. If you do, I'll attach it to the warning in your file.

- The purpose of this warning is to inform you of performance issues and to provide the opportunity for improvement.

- The details of the performance problem are . . .

- You (behavior) (when). The standard you violated is . . .

- The effect of this behavior is . . .

- This violation is not unprecedented. On (date) you (behavior). In response I (action taken).

- Your performance is expected to improve in the following ways.

- Failure to improve will result in further disciplinary action up to and including termination.

- If (behavior) happens again, the result will be . . .

Counseling Sessions That Accompany the Written Warning

- This meeting is a step in the disciplinary process. The purpose of this meeting is to discuss the problem and focus on how to improve as well as to inform you of the consequences of continued violation.

- We are having this conversation because I don't want to fire you. I'll fire you only if your actions give me no other choice.

- Please read the reprimand here before we proceed. I'll wait.

- Do you understand the issues?

- Do you really want this job?

- Explain why you broke the rule.

- What questions do you have about the document?

- Do you want to draft a response? If so, please have it to me within two days.

- We'll get a lot out of this meeting if we work together toward solutions. I'd like this to be a beginning, not an ending.

- You must meet your quota of (quota).

- You are expected to (expectation).

- Once this problem is corrected and performance is at acceptable levels for (time period), this action will be removed from your record.

- I'd like to hear your impressions of the warning.

- What do you see as the ideal outcome of this meeting?

- What can you do to improve your performance?

- I believe you know the policy, but I will explain it to make sure we both understand.

- You were given verbal warnings and (result).

- The policy says that in order to (protect safety, increase productivity, ensure the flow of communication, etc.) you need to . . .

- I need to enforce this policy because . . .

- What alternative do you think we have?

- We want you to be part of the team, which is why we want to work with you on this.

- I need someone to do your job, and I'm hoping it will be you.
- Let's start with facts. Then we can move into interpretation.
- Please sign here to verify that we had this conversation.
- Let me summarize what you said about the issue.
- Let's schedule a meeting in a month so we can talk about how things are progressing.

Perfect Phrases to Suspend an Employee

■ This meeting is for me to inform you that you will be suspended (when) until (when) because (behavior).

■ This suspension is (with, without) pay.

■ In review, we have given you verbal notice and a written warning with a counseling session. In those, you were informed that . . .

■ Normally we have a progressive policy of dealing with performance issues. This behavior is too egregious to allow that. I'm suspending you pending investigation.

■ Your performance plan was to (summarize plan). Your performance has not improved in the following ways (summarize discrepancy). If your performance does not improve after suspension, the next step is . . .

■ Your e-mail will be blocked and I need the keys returned as well as the company credit card.

■ This suspension is intended as an opportunity for you to decide if you really want to work here.

Perfect Phrases to Inform the Team About a Co-Worker on Suspension

- (Name) has been suspended until (date).

- Please do not contact (Name) regarding work-related matters. Until further notice, contact (Name).

- Out of respect for (Name)'s privacy, that is all the information I can provide.

- In order to cover (his, her) responsibilities we need to pull together.

- I'll need your help to keep things running smoothly.

- You may be curious about the circumstances. However, legally and ethically I am not able to disclose any information.

Perfect Phrases to Receive a Complaint

We need to take complaints seriously to avoid legal trouble. Make it easy for individuals to file complaints without fear of reprisal. For routine issues, see "Perfect Phrases to Encourage Employees to Resolve Conflict," in Chapter 5. For serious issues, use the phrases presented here.

- I am glad you brought this to my attention.

- I appreciate your coming forward.

- I need to find out what is going on, and anything you can tell me will be helpful.

- Everything you say will be kept confidential.

- If you get any sense of retaliation, please let me know.

- I take your complaint seriously and I will conduct an investigation.

- What happened? Who was involved? How did you react? When and where did this happen?

- Did anyone else witness it? Did you speak to anyone else about it?

- Do you know anyone else who might know anything about the incident?

- Do you know of any other similar incidents?

- What evidence is there?

- If anything at all comes to mind later, please let me know.

- Of what you have told me, what do you feel needs to be confidential?

Perfect Phrases to Inform an Employee of a Complaint

■ I have received the following complaint about your behavior from (team member, customer, etc.).

■ I'm waiting to draw conclusions until I have the facts and a bigger picture of what happened.

■ I've heard one side of the story. Tell me yours.

■ How would you describe what happened? When? Where? Tell me what you did and when.

■ How often has this happened? When did it first happen?

■ Who else was involved?

■ How do you feel about my investigating this?

■ I need to investigate to discover what happened. I will be talking to other people about this. Is there someone you think I should talk to?

■ What is your response to the complaint?

■ Can you think of a reason why the accuser would lie?

■ Could the employee who complained have misunderstood your actions and intentions?

■ How harmonious has your relationship with the complaining employee been? (Do not use this if the name of the complaining employee is kept private.)

■ Did anyone see it happen?

■ Did you tell anyone about the incident?

■ Do you know of anyone who might have information about it?

- Do you know about any evidence of the incident?

- I will be interviewing witnesses before I conclude. I will keep this confidential and trust you to do the same.

- Because of the severity of the complaint I will be suspending you (with, without) pay until I have completed my investigation.

- We are conducting an investigation of the complaint and we will file a report once we have completed the investigation.

- You may review the report before we determine what action to take.

- Because of the seriousness of the complaint we will transfer one of you until we can determine what happened.

Perfect Phrases to Investigate a Complaint by Interviewing Witnesses

When we investigate complaints, open-ended questions elicit as much information as possible. If we play dumb, we avoid influencing the responses.

- You have been identified as a witness for something that happened.

- I need to talk with you about something you may have seen or heard.

- What did you see or hear? When and where did this take place? Did you tell anyone about it?

- Did (the employee who complained) say anything about what happened?

- Did (the accused employee) say anything about the incident?

- Have you witnessed other incidents between (the employee who complained) and (the accused employee)?

- Have you heard these issues discussed in the workplace? When, and by whom?

- Have you ever had problems with (the employee who complained) or (the accused employee)?

- Did you and the (complaining, accused) employee discuss (the area of work the complaint is about, for example, invoices, weapons, taking equipment home)?

- Did you hear (the accused employee) and (the employee who complained) talking last week? What did you hear?

- Was (the accused employee) at the meeting last week? Did anything unusual happen?

- Did you see an incident between (the accused employee) and (the employee who complained) last week?

- What have you heard that leads you to that conclusion?

- Whom have you discussed this with and what did they say?

- Was anyone else there when that happened?

- Do you have any documentation or evidence?

- Did anyone else receive documentation?

- I've heard differently. Do you think the allegations I have heard are invented? Why?

- Why do you think others remember it differently?

- I expect this discussion to be kept confidential.

Chapter 14

Perfect Phrases for Performance Reviews

For many employees, *performance review* means a scary, unpredictable end-of-year review session with a manager who is out of touch with the tasks they perform every day. Some managers may feel the same way. To counteract this perception, I advocate interim reviews to address problems and issues before the official review. Managers who provide interim reviews find the final review to be a celebration of great performance because they've handled performance issues already. Then the final review becomes an opportunity to celebrate success and move forward.

These phrases apply to interim reviews as well as to the final reviews.

Perfect Phrases to Announce Performance Reviews and Recommend Employee Preparation

- Your performance review is scheduled for (date).
- To prepare, please review your performance goals over (time since previous review).
- Please review your job description and bring suggestions about how to update it.
- Please reflect on what goals you want to target for the next review period.
- I would like to meet with you for a performance evaluation (date, time). In the meeting I'll review your performance over the past (time frame). I invite you to review my performance as your manager.

Perfect Phrases to Set Expectations and Create Ease

- I know these reviews can be a bit nerve-racking. I get nervous about them too!

- It's not my job to criticize you, but to help you get better at what you do.

- I arranged to give you my full attention here.

- The purpose of this meeting is to take a look at where you are strong, where you could improve, where you want to go, and how to get you there.

- I also see these reviews as a chance for me to see how well I've been doing my job in supporting you.

- To make the most of this time, let's regard ourselves as partners in this meeting.

- One reason I like reviews is that they give me the opportunity to tell you what I appreciate about you. I get to sing your praises and you won't stop me.

- This review gives me the opportunity to help you achieve your goals.

- This review gives us the opportunity to address our concerns.

- What do you see as the best outcome for this meeting?

- This isn't a one-way lecture. Your participation is important because what we come up with together will be far better than anything I could come up with on my own. I'm here to learn from you and to invite you to learn from me.

Perfect Phrases to Review Past Performance

- Let's see how you did and how you want to do going forward.
- I'm holding my calls to give you my full attention.
- I have your records here.
- Let's review each job standard and goal separately.
- Let's see how your standards and your performance compare.
- Let's see how your goals and your performance compare.
- Your performance in (example) is exceptional.
- You're making a difference here by (example).
- I'm impressed by (example).
- Your standards in the area of (area) are (standard) and your performance was at the level of (performance).
- Your performance (met, exceeded, fell short of) standards by (measure).
- Your performance (met, exceeded, fell short of) your goals by (measure).
- Let's compare notes.
- What are you most proud of?
- I try to give consistent, ongoing feedback. To help me find out how well I'm doing that, I'd like you to start to see how well your thoughts match mine. What do you think you're doing well or excelling in? In what areas have you improved? In what areas do you need to improve?

Perfect Phrases to Address Poor Performance During the Performance Review

As a reminder, if we manage well between reviews, we won't need corrective phrases during them. Corrective phrases have more of a place in interim reviews. But if we haven't been consistent with those, we will need to use them in our final reviews too.

- Let's talk about the areas for improvement.
- What do you think of your performance?
- What areas would you like to improve?
- What area of your performance do you see as not being as strong as it should or could be?
- Do you think you are meeting your standards and goals? If not, why not?
- Given the standards, we need to look at your performance in the area of (area).
- Let's talk about your progress toward (goal).
- Here is where I see a need for improvement.
- You are expected to (expectation). Here is what you did (performance). That discrepancy has the impact on the company and your co-workers of (impact).
- Does this performance concern you as it does me? Why or why not?
- Are you surprised by this rating?

- Why do you think it's important to us that you bring your performance up to standards? Why do you think it's important to you? How do you think it impacts others?
- Is there anything unclear about the standards?

Perfect Phrases to Set Goals During Interim Meetings or the Performance Review

- Let's take a look at setting new goals.

- The best goals are collaborated goals.

- Where do you see room to do your job better than the standards call for?

- Although you are meeting job standards in the area of (area), I believe you are capable of more. Do you agree?

- How would it benefit the company for you to target a higher standard in that area? How can you see it benefiting you?

- What strengths do you want to develop?

- What specifically can you do to enhance those skills?

- Where would you like to be in five years?

- What skills do you want to develop immediately?

- I recommend you improve those skills by (recommendation). Do you have ideas of how to go about it?

- How would improving those skills directly enhance your job?

- I suggest we measure success by (metric). What would you recommend?

- This goal is set to be achieved by (date).

- Based on last year's results, is this a realistic goal? Are you willing to completely commit to it?

Perfect Phrases to Create an Improvement Plan

- Let's work together to create a performance improvement plan to bring your performance level up.
- I believe you can do a great job with help to make that happen. What help would that be?
- I am committed to your success. I will partner with you to make this happen.
- I support you 100 percent and will let others know where I stand.
- What training would help you with the skills you need?
- What coaching do you need from me?
- Am I giving you the resources you need to do your job?
- What are the obstacles toward being able to (performance standard)?
- Can you agree to this plan?
- Will you commit to this plan in writing?
- Let's review the effectiveness of this plan when we meet (date).

Chapter 15

Perfect Phrases for Ending Employment

When the appropriate coaching sessions don't bring positive results and standards remain unmet, or when an employee must be discharged for non-performance-related reasons, it is tough to find the words. In the case of a performance-related termination of employment (note: *not* termination of the employee!), if we've done our jobs, they already know. Make employment severance as quick and clean as possible, and preserve as much of the employee's dignity as you can. The conversation will have three parts:

1. Opening
2. Brief explanation
3. Closing

Perfect Phrases to Open the Severance-Due-to-Performance Meeting

- I am sorry it has come to this.
- I suspect you know what this meeting is about.
- Please sit down. We have come to a final decision regarding your employment.

Perfect Phrases to Explain the Situation of Severance Due to Performance

- We gave you warnings and your performance is still not at an acceptable level.

- In our prior meetings we outlined the standards you must meet to stay on with us and you haven't met them.

- Despite warnings, your performance has not reached an acceptable level.

- I am forced to terminate your employment.

- Today will be your final day of employment.

- The reasons for this are the ones we have discussed and that are on file.

- This decision is final. It was based on your inability to rebound from two unsatisfactory performance reviews.

Perfect Phrases to Open the
Severance-Due-to-Cutbacks Meeting

- It's hard for me to tell you this. I know it's harder for you to hear it.
- I wish it could be different, but I am not in control here.
- This is one of the hardest things I have to do.

Perfect Phrases to Explain the Situation of Severance Due to Cutbacks

- Budget cutbacks force the elimination of your position.

- Despite our efforts to avoid having to do this, your job has been eliminated.

- Sometimes reality requires me to let go of people I value. That's what is happening now. I have to terminate your employment effective immediately.

- I understand that (another company) is looking for people with your qualifications.

- HR has a few leads for other jobs.

- How can I help you pull resources together?

- Personnel will discuss your final pay and collect your office keys.

- Talk to me. I can't change it, but I can listen and understand.

Perfect Phrases to Reaffirm the Employee and Close the Meeting

- I wish this could have been resolved otherwise.
- I hope you find work that suits you.
- I sincerely wish you good luck in your next position.
- (Shake hands.) Good luck. Please contact (Name) if you have any questions about (your noncompete agreement, severance package, handing off work, COBRA, etc.).
- I will be happy to provide a reference stating (comments).
- As you know, we have procedures when employment is ended. I'd like to be able to let you take your time to tie things up, and the fact that I can't does not reflect how I feel about you personally.

Perfect Phrases to Answer Common Severance Questions

- These are the terms of your employment termination.

- Your last day is . . .

- Regarding bonuses you are eligible for . . .

- Regarding accumulated sick leave and vacation time you haven't taken . . .

- Regarding pension, profit sharing, and saving plans . . .

- You will receive your last paycheck on (date).

- You (will, will not) be eligible for unemployment insurance.

- Let's go over what I will say to prospective employers if we receive a signed release from them.

- We will notify you any time someone requests information.

- Let's go over what we'll tell your co-workers and clients about your no longer working at this company.

- Your medical and insurance benefits (will, will not) continue.

- We do require that you return company property such as a car, pager or cellular phone, and keys by (time).

- You (can, cannot) say good-bye to everyone before you go.

- The way for you to go to your work area to get your personal things is (guidelines).

- You have the (hour, day, week) to gather your belongings.
- We (do, do not) want you to complete pending projects.
- To pass on your work to other employees, we ask that you . . .
- Whatever questions remain after today can be directed to . . .
- We will handle your pending appointments by . . .

Perfect Phrases to Tell the Workforce About an Employment Termination

- (Name's) employment has been terminated effective . . .
- To protect privacy, I won't go into details.
- If any of you has concerns about this, we can discuss them privately.
- To cover (his, her) responsibilities we need to work together.
- I'll need your help to figure out how we can keep things running smoothly.
- What suggestions do you have for handling this?
- Let's plan the transition.
- If this creates a particular hardship for any of you, please let me know.

Perfect Phrases for the Exit Interview

If an exit interview is for employment that ended in termination, it is best if someone who was not involved in the employment termination conducts it. Here are some phrases.

- The purpose of this meeting is to exchange information about your perception of the company and how it treats employees. We also want to tie up loose ends about the severance.

- Do you feel management communicates well?

- Is there anything you believe we should know regarding your experience here?

- What changes would help employees do their jobs better?

- What questions remain?

- Let's review the noncompete agreement.

- Have you returned all company items?

Perfect Phrases to Manage Remaining Employees After Layoffs

Statistics show that fewer than half of companies experience increased profits after layoffs.[1] This is largely attributed to the fact that surviving employees have a sense of demoralization and anxiety. While there isn't a panacea to instantly resolve the challenges of layoffs, good layoff management can help. Here are some phrases for that.

- The recent layoffs have increased everyone's workload, including mine. But I know this is the time we need to stay in sync with each other most. I will increase my availability through the transition by . . .

- I won't pretend things aren't tough. Here's what we're doing to weather the storm.

- Between the Internet and the rumors, you've heard or guessed about what's going on. Talk to me, and I'll tell you what I know and what I don't know, and if there are things I can't tell you yet, I'll admit it to you.

- I don't know what we will do about (situation), but I'll let you know as soon as I do.

- I understand the layoffs have created trauma and disruption, and while I'd like to pretend we can all get over it by Monday, I know the process takes time.

- I know it's weird to come to work and not see (Name) anymore. It will take time for all of us to adjust.

---

[1] Wendy Mack, *Leading After Layoffs*, Woodland Park, CO: Peak Publishing, 2009.

- It's hard to understand why we'd let someone as valuable as (Name) go. We did it because . . .

- If you have any more questions about why we laid (Name) off or how we're going to adjust, please ask.

- I can understand why you're angry about the layoffs.

- We're all anxious about the layoffs. Let's get clear about our direction so we can focus that anxiety into energy.

- I can't fix it, but I can listen.

- It's tough right now. I believe we're going to turn this around because . . .

- Let's lay our situation on the table and do some action planning as a team.

Chapter 16

Perfect Phrases for Virtual and Face-to-Face Meetings and Announcements

Meetings are tough enough to manage when everyone is in the room. When we lead virtual meetings, we have special challenges. New skills and habits will help us create clarity when meeting attendees can't see each other. We also need to teach attendees how to best communicate virtually.

Perfect Phrases to Start a Virtual Meeting

- This is (Name). Before we start with the agenda, I want to explain our telecommunication guidelines.

- Please give us your full attention. Just because we can't see you doesn't mean it doesn't matter if you do other things.

- Please be aware that there might be people listening whom you don't know about. Someone might have you on speakerphone where others in the office can hear.

- If you have questions before I open the floor, handle them by . . .

- I (invite, ask you to hold) questions as I present the main focus of the call.

- I will keep the phone lines open to encourage dialogue. If there is background noise, please mute yourself by . . .

- This is (Name). When you speak, please identify yourself, as I just did.

- If you're listening with speakerphone, please pick up the phone to speak.

- Does everyone understand what we are trying to accomplish today?

- (Name), how does that sound to you?

- Thanks, all of you. Does this make sense?

- We seem to be at an impasse. Let's take this (issue, topic) offline for additional work and discuss it again next week. I'll reach out to each of you individually over the next (hour, day, week) to discuss it more and get back to the group with a summary of the individual input. The next agenda item is . . .

■ Excuse me, team. We're all talking at once. Let's go around the table on this one. Let's each take thirty seconds to give input. (Name), I'd like for you to start.

Perfect Phrases to Start Both Virtual and Face-to-Face Meetings

The following phrases apply to starting both virtual and face-to-face meetings.

- The purpose of this meeting is to . . .

- The agenda covers the following points . . .

- (Name) will ensure we stick to the times allotted for each point.

- Please be brief.

- Please give the meeting your full attention. Tweeting and texting doesn't just distract *you*; it takes away from the entire group.

Perfect Phrases to Keep Meetings on Track

One of the biggest complaints people have about both virtual and face-to-face meetings is that they go on too long and are unproductive. Use these Perfect Phrases to keep your meetings on track.

- That's outside the scope of this meeting. Let's table that discussion and get back on target.

- That's not why we're here today. Let's return to the main focus of today's meeting.

- We'll schedule that for another time.

- We're beginning to lose sight of the main point.

- That is off topic. If it really is a pressing issue, we can accommodate it by tabling our discussion of (item). Do we want to do that?

- What do we need now to make a decision?

- Are we ready to decide?

- We have ten minutes. What do we need to do to accomplish our goals in that time?

- That's all the time we have today.

Perfect Phrases to Emphasize a Point

Pay careful attention to my next point. When we make points we really want people to remember, a simple phrase for emphasis can drive the point home. Here are a few.

- Pay careful attention to my next point.
- The key point is . . .
- If you remember one point, remember this . . .
- Listen carefully to what I am about to say.
- Here is the main point.
- This is particularly important.
- Here is what matters most.
- Here is an interesting fact.
- Everyone, please write this down.
- This next point is critical.

Perfect Phrases to Handle Interruptions

- Excuse me, I wasn't done yet.
- Let me finish. I'm almost done.
- Hear me out, and I will do the same for you.
- Just one more minute and I'll be done.
- Allow me to complete my point.
- I want to hear your point after I have completed mine.
- Hold that thought until I've completed mine.

Perfect Phrases to Solicit Opinions

- What do you think about this proposal?

- Would you like to add anything, (Name)?

- Who else has something to contribute?

- What's the best way to get this done?

- If you did have an objection to this initiative, what would it be?

- What other comments are there?

- Please tell me what you like about this (plan, procedure, idea, etc.).

- What would make you like this plan more?

- What could conceivably go wrong with this in the worst possible scenario?

- What do you think of this? I'm looking for fodder, not answers.

- Do you see a better way of doing this?

- What have I overlooked?

- Let's go around the room and ask at least one question each. If we are making any assumptions, let's find out now.

- I want to make sure my instructions are clear. What is your understanding of what I just said?

- What did I leave out?

- What would you like reviewed?

- What do you recommend our first step to be?

- Take a moment and summarize our discussion so far.
- What main points stand out in what we said?
- Let's see if I communicated well. What did you hear me say?
- We (I) can't do this alone. Your input is crucial.
- I need to hear from those of you who have not spoken yet.

Perfect Phrases to Comment on Opinions

- I never thought about it that way before.

- Good point!

- That's an option. I'd like to get some more to work with, though.

- I get your point.

- I see what you mean.

- Tell me more.

- What else?

- Exactly!

- Very insightful.

- I have to agree with (name of participant).

- Up to a point I agree with you. What I question is . . .

- I can see why you see it that way, but have you considered . . . ?

- Explain to me how that can work.

- I don't see what you mean. Could we have some more details please?

- I'm listening to you but I don't understand. What do you mean by . . . ?

- That wasn't what I was looking for, but it is an excellent point.

Perfect Phrases to Correct Information

- I can tell I wasn't clear.
- I need to clarify.
- That's not the point I intended.
- That's not what I meant.
- Let me state it another way.
- Let me say this.
- There seems to be a misunderstanding here.

Perfect Phrases to Focus Decisions

- How do we turn that into action?
- What do (you, we) need to decide?
- In order for me to decide, I still need . . .
- What do you suggest we do about this?
- What do you conclude from that?
- What do you see as the next step?
- If you had to choose a course of action now, what would it be?
- What do we want to have completed by our next meeting?

Chapter 17

Perfect Phrases to Empower the Team

I say that successful managers make themselves obsolete. I also say that a really good manager is one who can go on vacation without needing to field phone calls to fight fires. That happens when staff is empowered to do their jobs autonomously. I have included acknowledgment and appreciation phrases in my empowerment section because appreciation is a huge empowerment tool. Perfect Phrases that empower help us express appreciation, motivate employees, and help our teams do their jobs independently.

Perfect Phrases to Show Appreciation

- When you did (action), it made my job easier because . . .
- I am thrilled that you took care of that without my having to get involved.
- You handled that so well I'm feeling unnecessary—and that's a good thing.
- My formal job is to oversee you, but it seems like my real job is to congratulate you.
- I would have missed that had it not been for you.
- Your idea made the difference because (reason).
- This (report, project, etc.) is exceptional because . . .
- That was true genius.
- I am impressed by (action) because . . .
- I like working with you because . . .
- I can tell you are skilled with (skill set) by the way . . .
- I respect your mastery of detail in how you . . .
- You worked hard and you did it!
- I respect your deep understanding of . . .
- Thank you for consistently going out of your way to . . .
- Your professionalism is shown by . . .
- The time and thought you put into (project, initiative, etc.) is evident by the way you . . .
- You handled the details of (project) beautifully.
- I know it wasn't easy to (task) but you did it!
- You are an asset to the team because . . .
- You simplified this process in ways I never imagined.

Perfect Phrases to Motivate

- You have the power to make this happen.

- This is not something just anyone could do, but I know you can.

- I can see the skills you'll acquire from this task being valuable for you throughout your career.

- The job you do on this will help us fulfill our mission and vision.

- If you give it your best, I see two outcomes: growth and success.

- Take this on like you can't fail and know I'm here cheering you on.

- I see what you accomplished last quarter, and I get very excited to imagine what you can do going forward.

- Here is what we are facing, and it's up to us to turn it around. I believe we can.

- I am confident in our ability to overcome this issue and be stronger for having done so.

- If this were easy, everyone would do it. Everyone is not doing it, and we are. I'm proud to be on a team like this.

- I am committed to your success.

- Let's focus on what we want rather than what we don't want.

- I know we can create the future we want. We just need to agree what that is.

- Just because it hasn't been done does not mean we can't do it.
- We can find a better way.
- I always appreciate your way of looking at things.
- I'm optimistic about what we will accomplish.
- This company's future is in our hands.

Perfect Phrases to Empower Audibles and to Create Autonomy

- Your input is important to me. How would you solve this?

- I'd like your input before I make my decision.

- I find most employees are too busy trying to figure out what I want rather than figuring out what doing a good job means. What I want is for you to figure out what doing a good job means, even if that means renegotiating your job description.

- Please bring me two or three possible solutions and we will decide this together. It's true I am the manager, but I would not want to implement a solution that doesn't work for you.

- If you were the manager, what would you suggest?

- What have you tried so far?

- I want you to stretch the boundaries of your job.

- What have you done yourself to eliminate the obstacles?

- How does it appear to you?

- This is a decision you can make without consulting me.

- We've set the plan, but use your judgment if you need to call an audible.

- How would you handle this situation if I weren't available?

- If I'm not available and things change, call an audible.

- Have you applied all the guidelines yourself before bringing this to me?

- If you *did* know how to handle the situation, what would you do?

- How have you handled this in the past?

- I appreciate how you handled that one on your own.

- In the future I would like you to make your own decisions about (area).

- We have a budget of (amount) for this project. I trust you to decide how to apply it.

Chapter 18

Perfect Phrases to Communicate Up the Ladder

Most managers have managers of their own. This chapter helps us stay in sync with our managers, disagree with our managers, support our staff with our managers, keep our managers informed, and present new ideas.

Perfect Phrases to Stay in Sync with Your Manager

- Are you satisfied with what I've accomplished so far?
- How would you like for me to update you?
- Did this conversation go the way you hoped it would?
- It's hard to forecast how I'm doing as we approach my review. Is there anything I can do to meet your requirements?
- If you'd copy me on e-mails to (Name), it will help me stay in sync with you.
- I'd like to be included in meetings with (Names) so I have a deeper understanding of the decisions you make. Is that an option?
- I'd like to meet with you daily, if only for two minutes to have a check-in to align ourselves with each other. Can we arrange that?

Perfect Phrases to Disagree with Your Manager

There are times when we feel so strongly about a management decision we are compelled to speak out. How do we stand up for what we believe without performing career suicide?

These Perfect Phrases to disagree with our managers do carry risk. No matter how tactful we are, we could get labeled a troublemaker or worse. As in any situation, weigh the pros and cons before disagreeing. However, know that the greater the risk, the more you stand to gain. The strongest managers do what they believe is right, even when there is a risk involved. Here are some phrases to help.

- I am uncomfortable with this based on our mission statement and company values. I'd like to consider other options.

- While I'm sure you considered mission and vision when this decision was made, it strikes me as inconsistent with our company commitment. How are they integrated?

- I have always been proud to say that my company follows its mission and adheres to its values. I have some serious concerns about what we're doing now. Do you see this as in line with our mission and values?

- I feel strongly about this. I love this company and have always seen it as fair and ethical. I don't think this fits our usual standards.

- I need to resolve something to be able to do this in good conscience. Is what we're doing in line with our company values and ethics?

- Help me understand how you reached that conclusion.

- I wonder if we have the same information. My information leads me to a different conclusion.

- I want to give my best here. I can support you better if we can resolve these differences first.

- I want to be clear here. I am sincerely concerned about the direction we're heading.

- I am a team player, I enjoy my job, and I intend to stay here. However, I think we should reconsider this decision because (risks).

- I have a problem with this. I believe this is a flawed initiative for reasons I would be happy to outline. What are my options?

- I can see the short-term advantage of this decision. Let me outline the long-term concerns I have.

- I am concerned that if we continue on this path we could all end up in legal trouble.

Perfect Phrases to Warn Your Manager of Developing Problems

Since we have a different relationship with the workforce culture than our own managers do, we might know implications of decisions that he or she might miss. Here's how we talk about those implications.

- There are some things I need to tell you about the ground reality that is affecting implementation of our strategy.

- I don't want you to be blindsided, so I have a heads-up about trends I see.

- There is a buzz in the grapevine I need to discuss with you.

- I think you need to have a sense of what people are saying about (project, decision, etc.).

- This initiative isn't playing out the way upper management thinks it is.

- Things look different on the ground than they do from a distance. Here's what I think you should know.

- I've been monitoring social media for the buzz about our change initiative and there are some things I need to bring to your attention.

Perfect Phrases to Focus Priorities and Decline a Manager's Request

Sometimes we need to say no when our managers ask for things. These phrases help us do that in ways that don't come across as uncooperative.

- I understand this is important. I'm working on (project). Is this new project more important?

- What would you like me to set aside that I'm working on now to do this assignment?

- I'm flattered that you asked me. I'm not the best person for the job because (reason).

- Doing this now means I won't get (project) done by the deadline. Is that acceptable?

- Ordinarily I would say yes immediately. I'm on vacation next week and don't know that I can complete the project by then. Do you want me to start it anyway?

- I want to say yes. Right now I'm working on three projects for other people. Could you check with them to make sure it's appropriate to put their work aside to complete this for you?

- I would like to do it. I'm pretty swamped right now. Will you help me prioritize my other projects so we can see where this fits?

- With everything I have on my schedule, I can't give this project the attention it deserves. Is there someone else who can take over?

Perfect Phrases to Handle a Difficult Manager

Difficult supervisors range from micromanagers to managers who never give credit to directors whose aggressive tendencies are downright offensive. While it is risky to challenge a difficult manager, many people find that standing up to a manager is not only possible but necessary.

Perfect Phrases to Manage a Micromanager

If our managers seem overly involved in the details of our work, it might indicate a lack of trust, or it could be intended as support. Use Perfect Phrases to address the issue.

- I appreciate your attention to detail because I am also very detail-oriented. Are you uncomfortable letting me do this myself?

- When you change small words in my letters, I feel you don't trust me to do my job. How can I win your trust to work with more autonomy?

- I respect your need to be updated on how the project is progressing. If I give you a (daily, weekly, monthly) update, I believe that will give you the information you need and eliminate interruptions throughout the day. Would that work for you?

- I am accustomed to working autonomously. While I appreciate your support, I think it would be a better use of both of our time if we move me toward autonomy in a way that is comfortable for you. Do you have suggestions on how we can do that?

- I'd like to define my work more by outcome than by steps. Would that work for you?

- I like to function independently. If we could schedule check-in meetings, it would help us both be more productive. Are you open to that?

Perfect Phrases to Manage a Distrustful Supervisor

If there is an underlying sense of distrust from a manager, it usually helps to address it directly and resolve it if possible.

- I believe part of my job is to help you look good. Do you trust me to do that?

- I want you to be confident that I'm doing my job. What can I do to gain that confidence?

- I think we both have the same goals. We just have different ways of going about achieving them. Can we talk about our common goals?

- Are you concerned that I'll make mistakes?

- Are you concerned that I want your job?

- We seem to be working at cross-purposes rather than together. What can I do to help change that?

Perfect Phrases to Manage an Angry Manager

Sometimes it's best for us to deflect our own manager's anger. However, if our manager's behavior slips into bullying, we probably need to stand up to him or her. Here are phrases for both.

- Let's take an objective look at the data and see if we can come up with some answers.

- I want to do the best job I can and to have the best relationship with you possible. I am embarrassed when my errors are brought up in public. When I make errors in the future, let's discuss them in private.

- I would be very happy to discuss this with you in private.

- I heard you say that (accusation). Did I hear you correctly?

- I can get your point without (sarcasm, yelling, etc.).

- That is a serious allegation. I would like the facts that led you to that conclusion.

- Exactly what do I say or do that leads you to believe that I (accusation)?

- I will be happy to discuss this when we both are calm.

- I am a professional and I expect to be treated as one.

- I react better to requests than criticism. What are you asking me?

- I'd like to arrange a meeting with a third person so we can discuss your perceptions and figure out how we can be comfortable working together.

Perfect Phrases for Going Above Your Manager's Head

There are times to go above our manager's head. Unless we sense danger, protocol suggests we request permission or at the least inform our managers of our intentions.

- Would you be OK with my bringing this up with your manager?

- If we can't resolve this ourselves, I intend to take it to your manager. My hope is that we can work it through without that.

- We are at an impasse on this. It is important enough to me that I intend to bring it to the attention of your manager. Do you want to go with me or do you prefer that I do it alone?

- I want to go on record as being opposed to this decision. I intend to do that by sending a letter to your manager. I am telling you so you won't be blindsided.

- As you know, I am entitled to file a grievance on this issue. I prefer not to, but if it continues, I intend to do that.

- I would be happy to discuss this before a review board or mediating organization for unfair employment practices.

Perfect Phrases to Bring Ideas to Your Manager

Sometimes it's hard for us to get our own manager's attention when we want to share an idea. Other times we can get his or her attention, but we risk the manager taking credit for our ideas. You may not mind giving up credit, but if you do, there are ways to phrase your idea that will decrease the likelihood of that happening. Here are your phrases for sharing ideas.

- I have an idea that is different from what we have been doing. I'd like you to consider how it might work before you consider the reasons why it won't.

- I have an idea I ran past three other managers, and they all suggest I bring it to you. When can we meet to discuss it?

- Something you said the other day got me thinking . . .

- I'd like your opinion about what I did with some concepts you and I discussed last month.

- I have been considering how to increase my department's bottom line, and I have come up with a way to do it.

- Are you open to a suggestion?

Perfect Phrases to Break Bad News to Your Manager

- I just made what might be a career-limiting move.

- I have bad news and good news. The good news is that I have a plan of action to deal with the bad news, which is . . .

- I need to tell you about an error that I am responsible for and will correct.

- If wisdom comes from mistakes, I just gained a huge amount of wisdom.

- I made a miscalculation that I need to tell you about. Please remember my overall performance and years of improved service when I tell you what happened.

Perfect Phrases to Support Your Staff When You Report to Your Manager

Our effectiveness depends on our ability to balance our responsibility to our team with our responsibility to upper levels and to maintain the trust and confidence of both. Some managers are so eager to please upper levels they promise unreasonable outcomes that compromise the people they supervise. Some managers take credit for employee ideas. Some managers are loyal to employees to a point that keeps them from being responsive to the needs of the organization. Our managers and our employees need to know they can count on us. When we talk to our managers, these Perfect Phrases help us to support our team.

Perfect Phrases to Protect Your Team from Unrealistic Expectations from Your Manager

- Let me check with my staff to see when they can have it done. I will get back with you by noon today with a realistic deadline.

- The team is working very hard to meet the existing standards. It would extend them unrealistically to add this initiative.

- I appreciate the objective of these new measures. I believed they were unrealistic and put an unreasonable burden on the staff, so I did research to determine standard output of a department like ours. What I found is that we are already at a work level that is higher than average.

■ I would rather underpromise and overdeliver. We can have it done by (date).

■ I know we have worked miracles for you many times in the past. But we can't continuously work under that kind of pressure. A realistic turnaround time is (time).

■ If you are committed to this initiative, we will give it our best. I need to warn you of the risks involved by adding this to our current workload.

Perfect Phrases to Protect Your Team from an Inadvisable Layoff

■ I believe laying off (Name) would be a mistake because . . .

■ I appreciate the need to cut costs. I believe laying off (Name) would actually add to the cost because (reason).

■ If we need to cut costs, instead of laying off (Name) could we (suggestion) instead?

Perfect Phrases to Represent Your Team with Your Manager When Expectations Are Not Met

■ I know this didn't turn out the way we projected. I have a great team. I will talk to them and find out what happened.

■ My team is my responsibility. It is not their failure; it is mine. I will get back to you by the end of the week with what went wrong.

■ I'd like to remind you of our great track record when we talk about how we fell short this time.

■ My team has been working with the handicap of (limitation). If I believed we fell short of expectations here because of our own failings, I would tell you so. In this case, I think the issue is with the expectations, not with the team.

Perfect Phrases to Give Due Credit to Your Team When Speaking to Your Manager

When we give our staff or team due credit for successes, we get loyalty and hard work in return.

- Thanks for the compliment. I'd love to take the credit, but I can't. My team deserves the praise.

- Thanks for the pat on the back, but I didn't do it alone. My team did the work. I'll pass along your compliments.

- We really pulled together on this.

- Thanks. This couldn't have happened without (Name) doing (action) and (Other Name) doing (action).

Chapter 19

Dynamized Management Communication Can Energize Productivity

Dynamized management communication can explode productivity. It can cut through obstacles that drain energy and get your staff working energetically in alignment with each other and with you. That fuels output better than coffee does. (And I do love my coffee.)

When your thinking gets stuck, maybe you're thinking too small. When your team collides, maybe they're really out of sync. When your meetings can't compete with text messaging, maybe your wording needs succinctness. When your team seems unmotivated, maybe they need a better "why" with their what, when, and how. If you find yourself having the same conversation you had last month, it might mean you need to try an approach you haven't used before.

Now is the time for the old rules of communication to relax and allow the new dynamics to spring into action. The new style can and will revolutionize and dynamize your rapport and your experience as a manager. So be gracefully assertive, personalize, speak concisely, synergize, and dynamize. But most of all, let your management style express your best self and inspire those around you.

These hundreds of ready-to-use and ready-to-adapt phrases will help you find the perfect words to say what you mean and get the results you want.

About SpeakStrong Inc.

SpeakStrong's mission is to work with individuals and leaders at every level who have moved beyond victimhood and power games and seek to liberate their thinking and communication from remaining vestiges of limitation and contention, and to empower magnetic influence based on confluent communication and reciprocal engagement.

SpeakStrong offers a variety of tools, including a free online communication style inventory at **speakstrong.com/ inventory**.

About the Author

Meryl Runion is a Certified Speaking Professional with the National Speaker Association and the president and CEO of SpeakStrong Inc. She has written seven books that have sold over a quarter million copies worldwide. She loves words, clarity, and communication and is committed to finding the best words to communicate in ways that enhance relationships and joyful, productive living. Her (pretty much) weekly newsletter "The New Dynamics of PowerPhrases" provides practical tips for handling common communication challenges and is available at speakstrong.com. You can also interact with Meryl on her blog, submit your own PowerPhrases, and get ideas to address your individual communication challenges.

Meryl's clients include hundreds of corporations, associations, and governmental entities such as IBM, the IAAP, and the U.S. Army, as well as forward-thinking individuals.

You can reach Meryl at MerylRunion@SpeakStrong.com; 719-684-2633.

Follow her on Twitter: @merylrunion.

Other Books by Meryl Runion

PowerPhrases!

How to Use PowerPhrases to Say What You Mean, Mean What You Say, and Get What You Want

How to Say It: Performance Reviews
Perfect Phrases for Developing Dynamic Leaders
SpeakStrong

These books are available on the SpeakStrong website.

Keynotes and Seminars

Dynamized Management Communication: Interaction, Empowerment, and Productivity

Developing Dynamic Leaders: Inspiring Employees to Take Charge, Embrace Innovation, and Challenge the Status Quo

The New Dynamics of Communication: How to Influence, Lead, and Succeed in a Dynamized World

The Right Phrase for Every Situation...Every Time

THE IDEAL PERFORMANCE SUPPORT SOLUTION FOR MANAGERS AND SUPERVISORS

With over 30,000 phrases, *Perfect Phrases for Managers* is an unmatched digital resource that provides managers at every level with the skills they need to effectively manage any situation.

From performance reviews to documenting problems, to motivating and coaching teams, to managing difficult people and embarrassing situations, this performance support tool will help your company create an environment for exceptional performance.

Go to **www.perfectphrases.com** to learn more about *Perfect Phrases for Managers* and how you can access:

- A "Things to Consider" section with hundreds of bite-size coaching tips
- Audio clips from actual conversations
- Strategies for opening up healthy communication

The right phrase for every situation, every time.

Visit www.perfectphrases.com to learn how your company can qualify for a trial subscription.